CHANGING YOUR WORLD

Leader's Guide

Maria Wiblin

Abingdon Press

CHANGING YOUR WORLD AND EVERYBODY ELSE'S

LEADER'S GUIDE

This book is printed on acid-free, recycled paper.

04 05 06 07 08 09 10 11 12—10 9 8 7 6 5 4 3 2

MANUFACTURED IN THE UNITED STATES OF AMERICA

Development Team
Jola Bortner
Rusty Cartee
Harriette Cross
Tim Gossett
Sharon Meads
Beth Miller
David Stewart

Editorial Team
Crystal A. Zinkiewicz, Senior Editor
Tim Gossett, Development Editor
Pam Shepherd, Production Editor

Design Team
Keely J. Moore, Design Manager
Kelly Chinn, Designer

Administrative Staff
Neil M. Alexander, Publisher
Harriet Jane Olson, Vice President/Editor of Church School Resources
Bob Shell, Director of Youth Resources

Contents

How to Use Faith in Motion

Leader's Guide

Information and Formation

Topic and Key Verse
This Life-to-Bible curriculum starts with important topics for junior highs and goes to God's Word.

Take-Home Learning
The goal for the session is clear.

Younger Youth and The Topic
Find out more about your youth and how they are likely to connect with this concern.

Theology and The Topic
How does Christian faith and tradition help us to understand and deal with the concern?

You and the Scripture
Our being formed as a Christian through Bible reflection and prayer is essential for our teaching.

Transformation

The ultimate goal: Youth will become more fully devoted disciples of Jesus Christ.

1

What the World Needs Now . . .?

Topic: Love, Peace, and Justice

Scripture: Micah 6:8; Luke 6:17-23, 27-36

Key Verse: "I say to you that listen, love your enemies, do good to those who hate you, bless those who curse you, pray for those who abuse you" (Luke 6:27-28).

Take-home Learning: Christians are called to bring the love of Christ to a hurting, broken world.

Younger Youth and the Topic

In Sunday school, we tell children stories about how Christ was sent to bring the love of God to the world and of how Christians can actively show this amazing love to the hurting world around us. But just because they have heard these stories does not necessarily mean that youth live as channels of God's love. Amid the pressures of the world, adolescents may find it hard to live out acts of love, compassion, and justice.

Youth are bombarded with messages saying that acts of love, acts that promote peace, and acts that encourage justice are weak or even unpatriotic. Younger youth need to learn that living by Christlike values is not weak and certainly is not easy. The concept of "loving your enemy" is difficult (or even ridiculous) for many youth. Pop culture does not provide youth with examples of loving ones enemies—nor do their peers. Rather, youth are told over and again that it is OK to laugh at and ridicule those whom they don't like or those who are different. Many adolescents routinely watch television shows and movies in which revenge and violence are shown as appropriate ways to solve problems. Youth must be reminded that God's call through Christ is first and foremost to seek love.

Theology and the Topic

Although our faith is firmly planted on the foundation of Christ, we live in a world where many values and concepts of righteousness and justice are contrary to Jesus' teaching. Jesus' message remains radical in our society, just as it was in his. Not only does Jesus call those listening to love one another (something even pop music promotes) but also to live a life of peace and justice, to love our enemies, and to serve others humbly. Jesus lived out his teachings and died making the ultimate sacrifice in the name of love and justice.

Leader's Guide

We discover what it means to live a life of justice and kindness by looking at those with whom Jesus spent time. Again and again Jesus chose to reach out to those who had been cast aside by the rich and powerful. He dined with sinners, spoke with women, made disciples of tax collectors and prostitutes, laughed with children, and touched those who were considered unclean. His stories revealed a God who loves extravagantly and surprisingly. He challenged the social status of the religious elite and declared instead that the meek, the poor, and the reviled were actually blessed. His actions consistently declared God's love for all people.

Jesus' example is an invitation to us to live as he lived and to love as he loved. We too can love the least and the lost, seek justice boldly, and demonstrate the peace of Christ to a world that often experiences the chaos of violence. We also can see the face of God in each person we meet, and through each of us, Christ blesses this hurting world.

You and the Scripture

Read **Micah 6:8** and **Luke 6:17-23, 27-36.**

Take time each week to reflect on Micah 6:8 as it relates to each session's theme. This week reflect on how we are called to practice justice and express love and kindness in every situation.

- Look closely at Jesus' Sermon on the Plain. How does Jesus instruct us to act?
- How are Jesus' words countercultural and revolutionary today?
- How do you go about living out on a daily basis the actions to which Jesus calls us?

Throughout these sessions, encourage your youth to examine their inward faith and connect this faith with outward actions that imitate Christ's model. Challenge your youth to make a real difference in the world. As you prepare, examine your inward faith and outward actions, and challenge yourself to make a difference. Ask yourself:

- Who are your enemies?
- Is there someone in need of prayer for whom you have trouble praying?

Reflect on these questions as you recite the Lord's Prayer.

8

Changing Your World And Everybody Else's

Overview Chart
Look here for the big picture of the session. Also note the key activities, just in case time is tight.

Jump Right In!
The opening activity engages youth as they arrive.

Experience It!
Learning activities give youth a common base for making new connections.

Explore Connections
What do the Scriptures have to say? What does this mean for my life? What is a Christian to do?

Take the Challenge
The learnings are not just for Sunday!

Encounter the Holy
Ritual and mystery, prayer and commitment change hearts.

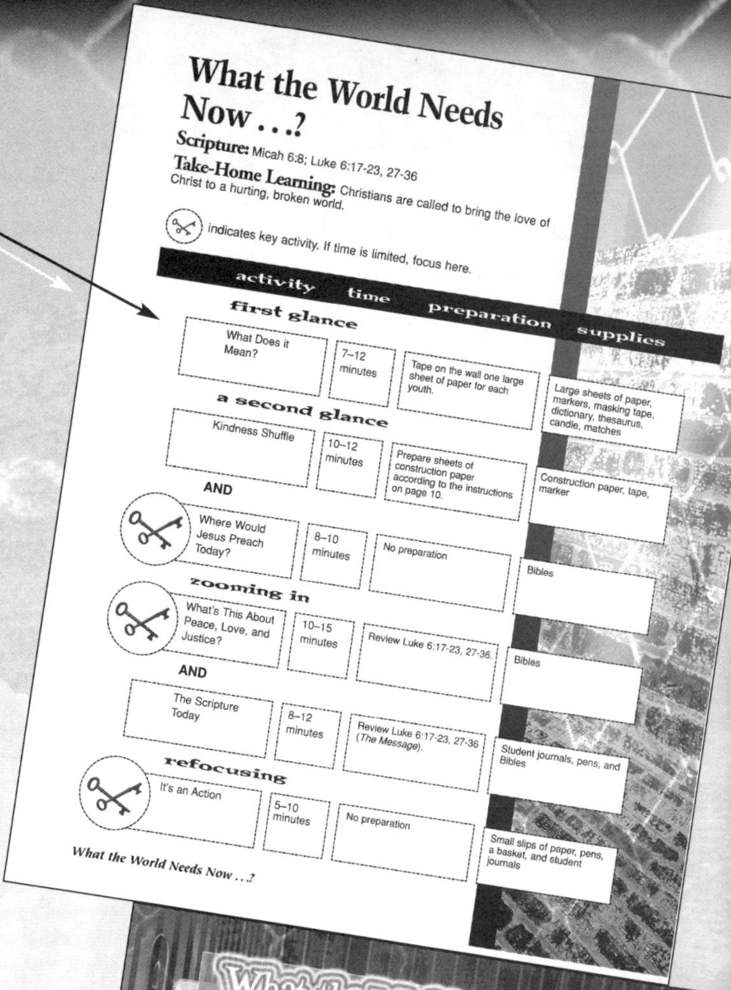

What the World Needs Now . . .?

Scripture: Micah 6:8; Luke 6:17-23, 27-36

Take-Home Learning: Christians are called to bring the love of Christ to a hurting, broken world.

indicates key activity. If time is limited, focus here.

activity	time	preparation	supplies
first glance			
What Does it Mean?	7–12 minutes	Tape on the wall one large sheet of paper for each youth.	Large sheets of paper, markers, masking tape, dictionary, thesaurus, candle, matches
a second glance			
Kindness Shuffle	10–12 minutes	Prepare sheets of construction paper according to the instructions on page 10.	Construction paper, tape, marker
AND			
(key) Where Would Jesus Preach Today?	8–10 minutes	No preparation	Bibles
zooming in			
(key) What's This About Peace, Love, and Justice?	10–15 minutes	Review Luke 6:17-23, 27-36.	Bibles
AND			
The Scripture Today	8–12 minutes	Review Luke 6:17-23, 27-36 (*The Message*).	Student journals, pens, and Bibles
refocusing			
(key) It's an Action	5–10 minutes	No preparation	Small slips of paper, pens, a basket, and student journals

What the World Needs Now . . .?

Student Journal and Reproducible Handouts

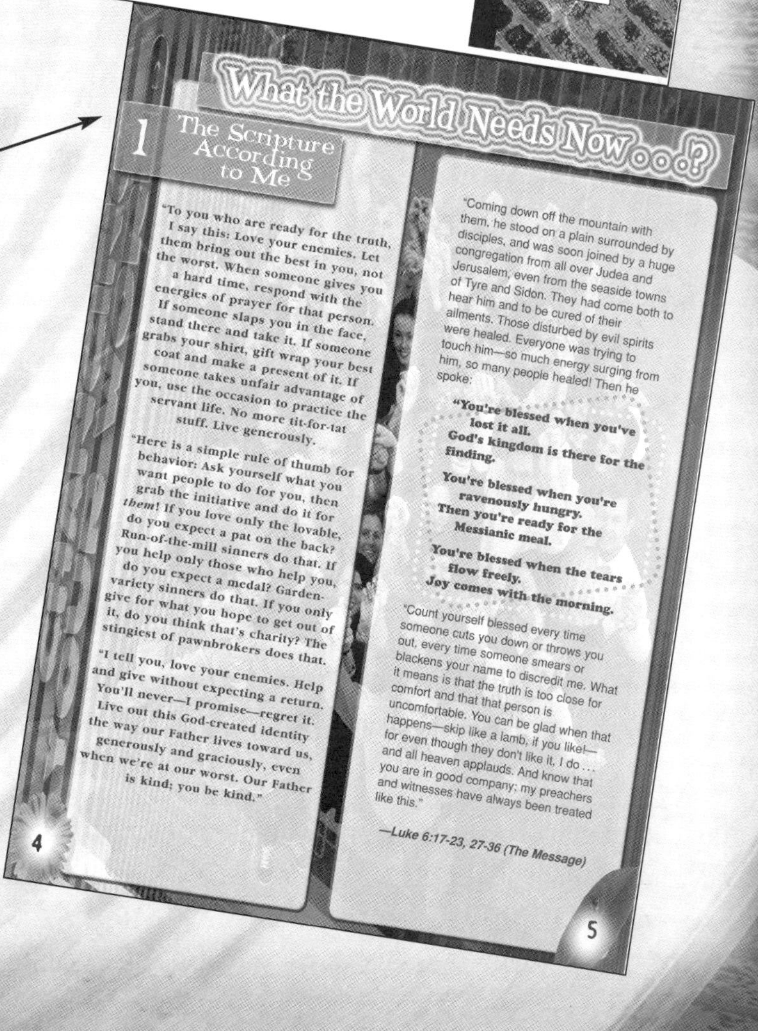

What the World Needs Now . . .?

1 The Scripture According to Me

"To you who are ready for the truth, I say this: Love your enemies. Let them bring out the best in you, not the worst. When someone gives you a hard time, respond with the energies of prayer for that person. If someone slaps you in the face, stand there and take it. If someone grabs your shirt, gift wrap your best coat and make a present of it. If someone takes unfair advantage of you, use the occasion to practice the servant life. No more tit-for-tat stuff. Live generously.

"Here is a simple rule of thumb for behavior: Ask yourself what you want people to do for you, then grab the initiative and do it for *them*! If you love only the lovable, do you expect a pat on the back? Run-of-the-mill sinners do that. If you help only those who help you, do you expect a medal? Garden-variety sinners do that. If you only give for what you hope to get out of it, do you think that's charity? The stingiest of pawnbrokers does that.

"I tell you, love your enemies. Help and give without expecting a return. You'll never—I promise—regret it. Live out this God-created identity the way our Father lives toward us, generously and graciously, even when we're at our worst. Our Father is kind; you be kind."

"Coming down off the mountain with them, he stood on a plain surrounded by disciples, and was soon joined by a huge congregation from all over Judea and Jerusalem, even from the seaside towns of Tyre and Sidon. They had come both to hear him and to be cured of their ailments. Those disturbed by evil spirits were healed. Everyone was trying to touch him—so much energy surging from him, so many people healed! Then he spoke:

"You're blessed when you've lost it all. God's kingdom is there for the finding.

You're blessed when you're ravenously hungry. Then you're ready for the Messianic meal.

You're blessed when the tears flow freely. Joy comes with the morning.

"Count yourself blessed every time someone cuts you down or throws you out, every time someone smears or blackens your name to discredit me. What it means is that the truth is too close for comfort and that that person is uncomfortable. You can be glad when that happens—skip like a lamb, if you like!—for even though they don't like it, I do . . . and all heaven applauds. And know that you are in good company; my preachers and witnesses have always been treated like this."

—*Luke 6:17-23, 27-36 (The Message)*

4 5

Life Focus
Topics deal with issues and concerns important to junior high youth.

Spirit Forming
The journal provides practical help and scriptural encouragement.

Group Friendly
Printed Scripture references, discussion questions, and handouts facilitate participation by individuals and small groups.

The Difference Is You!

Younger youth often are caught in the middle. Behaviorally they are not children, but they clearly are not on the brink of adulthood (as older adolescents are often described). Instead, they are on the brink of being on the brink—and in that realm, they are at times lost. Emotionally they may seem to be caught in a crossfire from one moment to the next, bouncing from happiness to sadness. Spiritually they are searching, perhaps wanting to test all that they have been taught.

Too often we place our focus on developing good Christian values in children, expecting that by late adolescence these values will be practiced. Between these times, our spiritual middle child may be neglected, much like the middle child in a family. The questions of life, Christian values, faith in the larger community, and what it means to be Christian all become real. To the shock and dismay of parents, these questions arrive earlier and earlier, and our spiritual middle child may be quick to verbalize these thoughts to anyone who will listen. As parents, teachers, youth workers, and pastors involved in a faith community and spiritual formation, our goal is to nurture these students and provide them with a safe environment to explore questions of faith as well as who they are while becoming mature Christians. It is also our task to provide challenging ways for them to live out their faith.

This study is designed to allow students to find relevant ways to make a difference in their world.

Each session in this study is designed to allow students at various stages of faith to dive into the Scriptures, to question, to spend time reflecting, and to find relevant ways to make a difference in their world. The topics provide springboards for Christian conversation, self-reflection, and opportunities to further strengthen the body of Christ.

In a task-oriented society where completion of the task is important and highly rewarded, allow God to work through each session, allow the discussions to go where they may, and leave "tasks" incomplete if necessary.

Focus on the following theme verse: "He has told you, O mortal, what is good; and what does the LORD require of you but to do justice, and to love kindness, and to walk humbly with your God?" (Micah 6:8). As you prepare, claim this Scripture, live with it daily, and allow the words to be alive in you.

What the World Needs Now ... ?

Topic: Love, Peace, and Justice

Scripture: Micah 6:8; Luke 6:17-23, 27-36

Key Verse: "I say to you that listen, Love your enemies, do good to those who hate you, bless those who curse you, pray for those who abuse you" (Luke 6:27-28).

Take-Home Learning: Christians are called to bring the love of Christ to a hurting, broken world.

Younger Youth and the Topic

In Sunday school, we tell children stories about how Christ was sent to bring the love of God to the world and of how Christians can actively show this amazing love to the hurting world around us. But just because they have heard these stories does not necessarily mean that youth live as channels of God's love. Amid the pressures of the world, adolescents may find it hard to live out acts of love, compassion, and justice.

Youth who grew up in a Sunday school program as children will have heard stories about how Christ was sent to bring the love of God to the world and of how Christians can actively show this amazing love to those who are hurting around us. But even those youth who were reared in the church might not live faithful to what they know to be God's way.

Amid the pressures of the world, they are bombarded with contradictory messages through television, movies, the Internet, and video games. Pop culture does not provide youth with examples of loving one's enemies—nor do their peers. Rather, youth are told over and again that it is OK to laugh at and ridicule those whom they don't like or those who are different. Many adolescents routinely watch TV shows and movies that depict revenge and violence as the way to solve problems. Although living by Christlike values is not being weak and certainly is not easy, youth must be reminded that God's call through Christ is first and foremost to seek love.

Theology and the Topic

Although our faith is firmly planted on the foundation of Christ, we live in a world where many values and concepts of righteousness and justice are contrary to Jesus' teaching. Jesus' message remains radical in our society just as it was in his. Not only does Jesus call those listening to

love one another (something even pop music promotes) but also to live a life of peace and justice, to love our enemies, and to serve others humbly. Jesus lived out his teachings and died making the ultimate sacrifice in the name of love and justice.

We discover what it means to live a life of justice and kindness by looking at those with whom Jesus spent time. Again and again Jesus chose to reach out to those whom the the rich and powerful cast aside. He dined with sinners, spoke with women, made disciples of tax collectors and prostitutes, laughed with children, and touched those who were considered unclean. His stories revealed a God whose love is amazingly extravagant. He challenged the social status of the religious elite and declared instead that the meek, the poor, and the reviled were actually blessed. His actions consistently declared God's love for all people.

Jesus' example invites us to live as he lived and to love as he loved. We too can love the least and the lost, seek justice boldly, and demonstrate the peace of Christ to a world that often experiences the chaos of violence. We also can see the face of God in each person we meet, and through each of us, Christ blesses this hurting world.

You and the Scripture

Read **Micah 6:8** and **Luke 6:17-23, 27-36.**

Take time each week to reflect on Micah 6:8 as it relates to each session's theme. This week reflect on how we are called to practice justice and express love and kindness in every situation.

- Look closely at Jesus' Sermon on the Plain in Luke 6:17-23. How does Jesus instruct us to act?
- How are Jesus' words countercultural and revolutionary today?
- How do you live out on a daily basis the actions to which Jesus calls us?

Throughout these sessions, encourage your youth to examine their inward faith and connect it with outward actions that imitate Christ's model. Challenge your youth to make a real difference in the world. As you prepare, examine yourself in the same way and challenge yourself to make a difference. Ask:

- Who are your enemies?
- Do you have trouble praying for someone who you know is in need of prayer?

Reflect on these questions as you recite the Lord's Prayer.

What the World Needs Now … ?

Scripture: Micah 6:8; Luke 6:17-23, 27-36

Take-Home Learning: Christians are called to bring the love of Christ to a hurting, broken world.

(key icon) indicates key activity. If time is limited, focus here.

activity	time	preparation	supplies
first glance			
What Does It Mean?	7–12 minutes	Tape on the wall one large sheet of paper for each youth.	Large sheets of paper, markers, masking tape, dictionary, thesaurus, candle, matches
a second glance			
Kindness Shuffle	10–12 minutes	Check the FAITH IN MOTION Teaching Helps on *ileadyouth.com/resources* or prepare sheets of construction paper according to instructions on page 10.	Computer with Internet service, or construction paper, tape, marker
AND			
(key activity) Where Would Jesus Preach Today?	8–10 minutes	No preparation necessary.	Bibles
zooming in			
(key activity) What's This About Peace, Love, and Justice?	10–15 minutes	Review Luke 6:17-23, 27-36.	Bibles
AND			
The Scripture Today	8–12 minutes	Review Luke 6:17-23, 27-36 using *The Message* translation.	Student journals, pens, Bibles
refocusing			
(key activity) It's an Action	5–10 minutes	No preparation necessary.	Small slips of paper, pens, a basket, student journals

first glance

Provide large sheets of paper, markers, masking tape, a dictionary, a thesaurus, a candle, and matches.

Tape one large sheet of paper on the wall for each youth you expect. (Option: Provide one sheet for each of the following four words and suggest all youth write on those four sheets.)

- **Love**
- **Justice**
- **Peace**
- **Mercy**

Special Note: A prayer appears at the conclusion of the first activity in each session. Use this prayer to focus youth on each week's topic.

a second glance

Provide construction paper, tape, and a marker.

If you have access to a computer with Internet service and use Microsoft Word, print out this activity from *ileadyouth.com/resources* FAITH IN MOTION Teaching Helps. Or write each of the words and definitions on separate sheets of construction or plain paper. Shuffle words and definitions, spread them upside-down on the floor or a table, and number 1 through 18 on the backs.

What Does It Mean? (7–12 minutes)

As the youth arrive, ask each to choose a large sheet of paper located near someone he or she doesn't know very well. Ask each person to write the following words on the paper, leaving space below each one: *Love, Peace, Justice, Mercy.* Then ask the youth to write as many synonyms (words or phrases) for each word as they can.

Allow youth a few minutes to work, then ask volunteers to read aloud the definitions of these words from a dictionary. Then have volunteers read aloud synonyms for each word from a thesaurus.

Divide the youth into groups of four or five. Ask group members to discuss the synonyms they listed. Ask:

- Which synonyms appeared on everyone's list?
- What was the most original synonym for love? peace? justice? mercy?

Gather the youth in a circle. (If you have a designated sacred space, gather in this area.) Place a "centering candle" in the middle of the circle. Light the candle and pray the following prayer. (Leave this candle lit throughout the session.)

Light of the world, shine in our hearts.
Illuminate the dark and barren corners of our lives so that we may see those things that keep us from our love for you.

Light of the world, shine in our midst that we might see more clearly the path on which you lead us and the life of love to which you call us. Amen.

Kindness Shuffle (10–12 minutes)

- **Patience:** the will or ability to wait or endure without complaint
- **Mercy:** an act of kindness, especially when shown to someone who deserves punishment
- **Empathy:** ability to share another's emotions, thoughts, or feelings
- **Love:** a deep and tender affection for or attachment or devotion to a person or persons
- **Humility:** absence of pride or self-assertion
- **Purity:** freedom from evil or sin; innocence
- **Joy:** a very glad feeling; happiness; great pleasure; delight
- **Courage:** an attitude of facing and dealing with (not withdrawing from) dangerous, difficult, or painful situations; being brave
- **Compassion:** sorrow for the sufferings or trouble of others accompanied by an urge to help; deep sympathy

Divide youth into two teams and have each team stand in a straight line. Alternating teams, have the youth at the front of a line choose two sheets of paper in an effort to find a match. Ask the student to read aloud both choices. If it's a match, tape the two sheets of paper to the wall. (You may want to designate a section of the wall for each team to post matches.) If not, they should replace the sheets of paper in their upside-down positions on the floor.

Ask each student to pick one of the qualities the world needs and explain why he or she chose that quality. As a part of the explanation, ask the youth to connect that quality with Jesus' life and teachings.

AND

Where Would Jesus Preach Today? (8–10 minutes)

Provide Bibles.

Divide the youth into groups of four or five. Say: "As a group, decide where you think Jesus would spend his time teaching and preaching if he were walking the earth today. Reinforce your answer with evidence from Scripture. Look through the Gospels to locate where he preached and taught during his lifetime. You may have more than one answer, but be sure you agree on the answers."

Hand out Bibles and allow youth five or six minutes to work. Then ask a volunteer from each group to present its answers to the others.

Then say: "Jesus isn't here to teach and preach among us. Instead we are responsible for spreading his message. The people Jesus sought out are the same people we should seek out; we are his hands, his feet, and his voice."

What's This About Love, Peace, and Justice? (10–15 minutes)

zooming in

Provide Bibles.

Hand out Bibles and ask one youth at a time to read one verse from Luke 6:17-23, 27-36 until the entire passage has been read. Then ask:

- To whom is Jesus speaking? (*Possible answers: the poor, the sick, women, children, and so on*)
- Why does Jesus' audience matter? (*Possible answer: Jesus spoke to persons who were ignored or cast aside by those in power; he ignored prejudices and stereotypes; his message was meant for all people, even those who were considered undesirable.*)
- In Matthew's account of this sermon, Jesus preaches on a mountain (The Sermon on the Mount). In Luke, Jesus preaches on a plain or a level place. What does this setting say about how Luke sees Jesus' audience? (*Possible answers: Everyone is on the same level; no one is above anyone else.*)
- What does this passage say about who your neighbors are and how you should treat them?

Provide student journals, pens, and Bibles.

Ask youth to paraphrase one of the following Scripture passages:

- **Luke 6:17-19**
- **Luke 6:20-23**
- **Luke 6:27-31**
- **Luke 6:32-36**

AND

The Scripture Today (8–12 minutes)

Ask a volunteer to read aloud Luke 6:17-23, 27-36 from *The Message* on page 5 in the student journal. Then ask:

- What was different about this translation? What was similar?
- Did this translation give you a different image of Jesus preaching than more traditional translations? How?

Hand out student journals and ask youth to rewrite portions of Luke 6:17–36 (see margin note) on separate sheets of paper. Encourage them to look at their Bible translations along with the translation from *The Message* as they rewrite. Allow sufficient time for youth to work, then ask volunteers to read aloud their paraphrases.

refocusing

Provide small slips of paper, pens, a basket, and student journals.

It's an Action (5–10 minutes)

Hand out pens and two or three small pieces of paper per participant. Ask youth to write on these sheets of paper active ways in which they can live out the gospel call to love, mercy, justice, and peace. Then ask them to fold their sheets of paper and place them in a basket.

Now divide the youth into pairs and have each select a piece of paper and act out the words or phrases for the others. Explain that they may speak but may not mention the words or phrases written on the slips of paper. Encourage remaining youth to guess the actions being performed. Schedule enough time for everyone to have at least one opportunity to act.

Then say: "All of you acted out ways to practice love, mercy, justice, and peace in your lives." Ask:

- Can we love without performing loving acts? Can we be merciful without showing mercy? Can we seek justice without working for it? Can we build a peaceful world without being peacemakers? Why?
- Which of these actions will you implement this week? Which of these actions could you make a regular part of your life?

Give the youth a couple of minutes to complete the activities on pages 6–7 in the student journal. Then close the session in prayer. Say: "Now each of you must go into the world, taking what you have learned and allowing the love of Christ to shine through your life and actions."

Do Something Before We Can't Breathe!

Topic: The Environment and Recycling

Scripture: Genesis 1:26-31a

Key Verse: "And it was so. God saw everything that God had made, and indeed, it was very good" (Genesis 1:30b-31a).

Take-Home Learning: God created us in God's own image, and we are to care for creation as God cares for us.

Younger Youth and the Topic

Have you ever wondered why some younger youth seem unable to think past today? Developmentally, many are still learning to think in the abstract, a necessary capability for thinking ahead. For many teens, long-term planning means looking ahead a week—a month at most. The idea of drastic changes occurring over a long period of time is difficult for youth to grasp. They can hardly imagine running out of resources such as oil or paper. The extinction of a species seems almost impossible, and youth have not lived long enough to notice a significant change in air or water quality. Some youth think recycling is a waste of time or is unrelated to their lives.

However, much of the Millennial Generation (persons born between 1982 and 1999) are deeply concerned about the future of our planet. They have studied global-warming statistics and concepts such as biodiversity and resource scarcity. Some have hands-on experience with issues such as water quality in their communities. As a generation, Millennials are expected to be more socially conscious than the Baby Boomers or Generation X, and their education is leading them to believe they can solve any problem.

You can help both groups of youth—those who are environmentally conscious and those who are not—to see that environmental responsibility is a matter of faith. Christians are called to be good stewards of their resources—including natural resources. Younger youth in particular require practical suggestions for taking care of God's creation, and they need to realize that reusing and recycling can be acts of faith.

Theology and the Topic

The Hebrew Scripture begins with a celebration of life and a theological framework for how we should think about our role within creation. God

Read **Genesis 1:26-31a**. What images come to mind? What words and phrases stick out?

Think about these images, words, and phrases while prayerfully reading the passage a second time.

created us in God's own image. God gave us life, and as part of that life, we received dominion over all of creation. Often we associate dominion with power, control, and even destruction. It is healthier for us to think of dominion as responsibility—responsibility to care for that which God has entrusted to us.

Remember that God concluded each act of Creation by saying, "It is good." If God considers all creation good, doesn't it follow that God would want it to remain that way? If we are created in God's own image, we are to care for creation as God cares for us.

You and the Scripture

As you prepare for this session, spend some time outside enjoying God's world. Try to find a quiet place nearby, such as a park, where you can be with God.

- Take time to look around. Look as if you haven't viewed God's creation before. What new sights do you see? Remember that God created all the trees, birds, sky, and grass—even those pesky mosquitoes.
- Now close your eyes. What do you hear? What do you smell?
- Take a deep breath. As you inhale, thank God for all of creation.
- Now release your breath and breathe in again. Thank God for creating you and caring for you.
- After you have offered a prayer of thanksgiving, take another look at the area around you. What seems out of place? Are there trees that need to be planted? Are there fewer trees now than before? Are there animals? Is there litter on the ground? How is the air quality?
- Consider your own place in the larger environment. Do you make intentional decisions and choices with creation in mind? Do you continually seek out ways to leave a smaller "footprint" on this planet? How does your faith and your responsibility toward creation affect the way you eat, shop, and live?

Do Something Before We Can't Breathe!

Scripture: Genesis 1:26-31a

Take-Home Learning: God created us in God's own image, and we are to care for creation as God cares for us.

(key icon) indicates key activity. If time is limited, focus here.

activity	time	preparation	supplies
first glance			
3 R's Relay	6–9 minutes	Prepare bags of recyclable items and recycling boxes or bins according to the instructions on page 16.	Bags of recyclable items, recycling boxes or bins, blindfolds, candle, matches
a second glance			
Environmental Match	5–10 minutes	Duplicate the Environmental Match handout on page 49.	Handouts, pens or pencils
AND			
(key) Take a Look	15–25 minutes	Duplicate the Take a Look handout on page 50. Consider enlisting adult helpers.	Handouts, pens or pencils
zooming in			
(key) Read the Word	8–12 minutes	Review Genesis 1:26-31a.	Bibles
refocusing			
An Action Plan	7–10 minutes	Arrange for adult volunteers to assist.	Trash bags, work gloves
AND			
(key) How Do I Care?	5–7 minutes	No preparation necessary.	Student journals, pens Optional: CD player and CD featuring environmental sounds

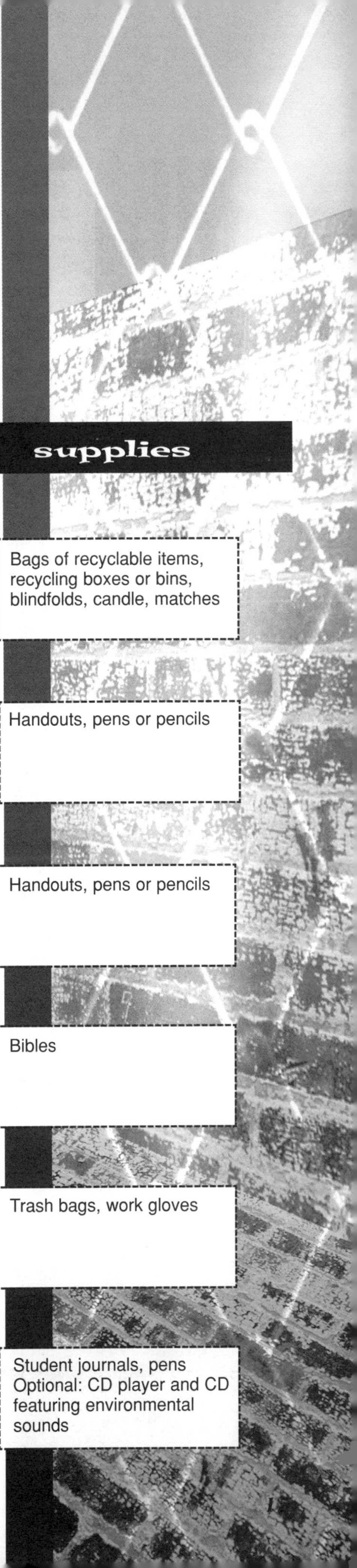

first glance

Provide one bag of recyclable items for each team, one recycling bin or box for each type of recyclable item, one blindfold for each team, a candle, and matches.

Be sure to recycle these items when you are finished with them!

a second glance

Provide copies of the Environmental Match handout on page 49 along with pens or pencils.

Leader's Guide

3 R's Relay (6–9 minutes)

Divide the youth into teams of three to five. Give each team a bag of recyclable items (*clean* aluminum cans, bottles, plastic containers, sheets of paper, and so forth) and a blindfold. Have each team line up behind its bag, and ask the first person in each line to wear a blindfold. At the other end of the room, place one recycling bin or box for each type of recyclable product.

Say: "I want you to recycle your entire bag as quickly as possible. I want the first person in line to reach into the bag, pull out one item, walk to the recycling area, and put the item in the correct bin. You may verbally direct your teammate to the correct bin. When the first person has dropped the item into the bin, he or she will walk back to the line, remove the blindfold, and hand it to the next person in line. The first team to recycle its entire bag wins."

Ask:

- Which of these items do you recycle at home?
- What could you recycle that you do not now recycle?
- Are there other ways to recycle besides collecting items and putting them in a bin? Explain. (*Possible answers: reusing clothing, using butter tubs to store leftovers, using old towels as cleaning rags, and so on*)
- What environmental issues most concern you? What do you do to help the environment?

Gather the youth in a circle. (If you have a designated sacred space, gather in this area.) Place a "centering candle" in the middle of the circle. Light the candle and pray the prayer below. (Leave this candle lit for the remainder of the session.)

Creator of light, shine in our hearts.
Illuminate the dark and barren places so that we may see those things that keep us from the love you have for us.

Creator of light, shine in our midst so that we might see more clearly the path on which you lead us and the life of love to which you call us. Amen.

Environmental Match (5–10 minutes)

Distribute copies of the Environmental Match on page 49 along with pens or pencils. Say: "Follow the instructions on the handout and collect as many signatures as possible. No person may sign your page more than three times."

After five minutes, ask:

- Who collected enough signatures to fill in all of the squares?

- Were there squares that you didn't understand? Which ones?
- What do all of these squares have in common?
- What does this activity have to do with faith?

AND

Take a Look (15–25 minutes)

Distribute copies of the Take a Look handout on page 50 along with pens or pencils. Instruct the youth to pair off, then ask: "Can anyone define the word *audit*?" (Wait for responses.) Then explain: "An audit is an in-depth review, usually related to how a business keeps its records. This morning we are going to conduct an environmental audit of our church. On the handout are issues we must consider in our effort to be an environmentally friendly congregation. You and your partner will have ten minutes to gather information. You may ask adults you see for help, but don't interrupt any Sunday school classes."

Provide copies of the Take a Look handout on page 50 along with pens or pencils.

Ahead of time you may want to "plant" knowledgeable adults around the church facility to help answer questions.

Set a return time before sending out pairs. When they return, have each pair compare its answers with another pair's. Then ask:

- How did the church do overall?
- What do these questions have to do with protecting God's creation?
- Why is it important for a church to ask itself these questions?
- What could we do as a group to help our church become more environmentally friendly?

Discuss ways to report information to the entire congregation.

Read the Word (8–12 minutes)

zooming in

Provide Bibles.

Hand out Bibles. Ask each youth to silently read Genesis 1:26-31a. Then ask: "What do you think this passage says about our relationship to God's creation?"

Ask the youth to close their Bibles and move to a spot in the room where they can be alone. Ask them to close their eyes, relax, and listen as you read aloud the passage. Instruct the youth to pay attention to sights, sounds, smells, and emotions. After reading the passage slowly and with feeling, ask:

- What did you hear as I read the passage aloud that you didn't notice when you read silently?

- In this Scripture, God refers to us as good. What does it mean for God to call us good?
- What does it mean for the rest of creation that humans are created in God's own image?

refocusing

Provide trash bags and work gloves.

Work gloves usually can be purchased in bulk at discount or hardware stores; use latex gloves as a last resort.

An Action Plan (7–10 minutes)

Divide the youth into pairs. Give a trash bag to each pair and work gloves to each person. Instruct pairs to walk around the church grounds and pick up any trash they find. (You might ask adult volunteers to supervise.) Also ask the youth to pay attention to where they find the trash. Allow five minutes for this activity. When the youth return, ask:

- Was this a new experience for anyone?
- What difference did we make as a group?
- What does it say about someone's view of creation if that person litters? if the person always throws away trash? if the person reuses and recycles as much trash as possible?
- How does cleaning up trash help us to live out our faith?

AND

Provide student journals, and pens. Optional: a CD player and a CD featuring environmental sounds.

Optional: If you own or can borrow a CD featuring environmental sounds, consider playing the CD while students work in their student journals.

How Do I Care? (5–7 minutes)

Hand out student journals and pens. Allow about five minutes for students to complete the activities on pages 8–11 in their journals. If time permits, allow youth to choose partners and discuss their answers. Close the session in prayer. Blow out the candle (lit in the opening activity) to signify that youth are to go into the world, taking what they've learned everywhere they go.

Just Because We're Different

Topic: Breaking Barriers and Overcoming Racism

Scripture: Acts 10:9-16, 28-35

Key Verse: "I truly understand that God shows no partiality, but in every nation anyone who fears him and does what is right is acceptable to him" (Acts 10:34b-35).

Take-Home Learning: God created our differences. How can we respect these differences out of love?

Younger Youth and the Topic

Younger youth strive to be like others their age. They actually avoid anything causing them to stick out in a crowd or that draws attention to the fact that they may be different from their peers. When learning that a friend is somehow "different," many youth find it easier to make fun of or ignore that friend than to be "different" by association. Even when youth try something new, their attempts often are based on what they've observed in pop culture. For many youth, being different still means being cool, doing what is "in," and being accepted by their peers.

Our task with students this age is to help them identify any barriers that may separate them from others and to work with God to eliminate these barriers. Your responsibility as leader is to provide a safe space where youth learn to treat one another as equals and overcome their stereotypes and attitudes toward individuals who are "different."

Theology and the Topic

God through Christ calls us to love and care for all persons regardless of barriers separating persons into groups based on financial status, educational level, race or ethnicity, nationality, religion, gender or sexual identity, and so on. Our differences have spawned disagreement, arguments, anger, and mistrust—all of which reveals our brokenness as children of God.

God calls us to love others as Christ loved us, looking into their hearts. In his day, Jesus broke down many of the barriers separating people: He associated with persons who were poor or sick. He ate meals with those who had questionable backgrounds. Some of his closest followers were unmarried women. The story of the good Samaritan challenges the idea that a person's goodness is related to a person's nationality.

But Jesus' message was not entirely new; he was building on the biblical tradition that strangers in our midst should be treated fairly. The story of Ruth, for example, tells of a woman who overcomes the social barriers related to her gender and ethnicity. Ruth was a Moabite and a widow who had the option of finding a new husband and living among the people of Moab. Instead she chose to step out of her comfort zone and to live with her mother-in-law amid an unfamiliar culture.

Simon Peter grew up believing that some animals were clean and others were unclean. In Peter's culture, it was proper to eat those animals considered clean and immoral to eat those that were not; unfortunately, Peter had come to view people in the same way: Some were acceptable, and others were not. But in a vision, God showed Peter that since all animals are created by God, all are clean. Likewise, all persons are acceptable and welcome in God's kingdom.

God values all persons and calls us to look for the possibilities within those who are different from us. We must set aside any notion that we—and those who are like us—are the only ones chosen by God. God expects us to show no partiality and to treat everyone equally.

You and the Scripture

Read and meditate on **Acts 10:9-16, 28-35.**

Pray for strength to face yourself and your prejudices.

We like to think that we are above prejudices and stereotypes, but most of us make judgments about others. We may judge a particular group of people such as the poor or overweight. Other times we may judge particular people—like the "crazy guy" who dresses strangely and mutters to himself as he walks around town.

Often we don't understand or even realize why we erect barriers or make the judgments we do. We need the guidance of the Holy Spirit to open our eyes to these divisions and help us learn to overcome them.

As you prepare for this session, ask yourself: *Do I judge specific individuals or groups?* Answer honestly and pray for strength to live a life of love, viewing others through the eyes of Jesus.

Just Because We're Different

Scripture: Acts 10:9-16, 28-35

Take-Home Learning: God created our differences. How can we respect these differences out of love?

(key icon) indicates key activity. If time is limited, focus here.

activity	time	preparation	supplies
first glance			
(key) "We're Not That Different" Shuffle	4–7 minutes	No preparation necessary.	Chairs, candle, matches
a second glance			
Who's In, Who's Out?	10–20 minutes	Prepare a nametag for each youth you expect. Divide the nametags into two groups and mark them separately.	Nametags, marker
zooming in			
(key) The Walls That Divide Us	8–12 minutes	No preparation necessary.	A sheet of paper long enough to stretch across the room, masking tape, markers
AND			
(key) Clean or Unclean?	5–10 minutes	Review Acts 10:9-16, 28-35.	Bibles
refocusing			
Journaling	5–10 minutes	No preparation necessary.	Student journals, pens or pencils
AND			
Sending Forth	4–6 minutes	No preparation necessary.	No supplies

first glance

Provide chairs, a candle, and matches.

Consider beginning the game yourself so that youth will learn something interesting or unique about you.

"We're Not That Different" Shuffle (4–7 minutes)

Ask for a volunteer to be "it." Direct remaining youth to sit in chairs in a circle. "It" should stand in the middle of the circle and call out something that is interesting or unique about him or herself. (The idea is to share a fact that might set apart "it" from the other youth such as "I like brussels sprouts" or "I've traveled outside of the country.") Everyone in the group who can identify with the youth in the center's unique quality or interest should stand up and find a different chair. When other people stand, "it" should quickly find a chair, leaving another youth standing. This youth moves to the center and repeats the process. Continue play until most of the youth have had an opportunity to stand in the center. Encourage youth to notice how many of their peers are like them.

Now gather the youth in a circle. (If you have a designated sacred space, gather in this area.) Place a "centering candle" in the center of the circle. (Leave this candle lit for the remainder of the session.) Light the candle and pray:

Jesus, Light of the world, shine in our midst. Illuminate the dark and barren places so that we may see one another through your eyes.

Jesus, Light of the world, shine among us so that we might see more clearly the love you showed us and the inclusive life to which you call us. Amen.

a second glance

Provide nametags and a marker.

Make a nametag for every youth you expect. (Provide extras in case you have visitors.) Divide the nametags into two groups—the *"in"* group and the *"out"* group. Give each group's nametag an identifying mark, but be sure the markings are not obvious at first glance. If necessary, make adjustments so that self-confident youth are in the "out" group and quiet or insecure youth are in the "in" group.

Who's In, Who's Out? (10–20 minutes)

Distribute the prepared nametags (see the note in the margin), then gather the youth in a circle and ask them to join hands. Choose one student from the *"in"* group to walk around the outside of the circle. Instruct that youth to try to enter the circle using any means necessary, so long as his or her feet remain on the ground (for safety reasons). Instruct remaining youth to do whatever they can to keep out the person trying to gain entrance to the circle.

Allow the person on the outside a minute or so to break in. Then choose another volunteer from the "in" group and repeat the process. After two or three rounds, select another youth from the *"in"* group and ask him or her to stand on the inside of the circle. Now give him or her the opposite instructions: Attempt to get out of the circle.

Ask the following questions, but only accept responses from the "in" group (without being rude to the "out" group):

- How was it challenging to keep someone out of the circle?
- How did it feel being excluded from the circle? How did it feel being trapped inside the circle?
- Have I ignored or overlooked anyone as we've done this activity? Why do you think this is?

Explain to the youth that you randomly divided them into "in" and "out" using markings on their nametags. Ask those in the "out" group:

- How did it feel to be ignored or overlooked just because of a marking on your nametag?

Say: "I paid attention to some of you and ignored others of you because I had put you into groups. Putting people into groups keeps us from treating one another as unique individuals with unique gifts. All of you are in my 'in' group, and I respect each of you as an individual. The only reason I would ever ignore any of you would be to make a point in a game like this one."

The Walls That Divide Us (8–12 minutes)

Divide the youth into two groups and have them sit on opposite sides of the table or the room. (Consider using your "in" and "out" groups from the previous activity.) Give each group an assortment of markers. Say: "Use your markers to draw bricks across the entire sheet of paper so that it resembles a brick wall. Draw the bricks fairly large and be careful not to tear the paper."

When the youth have finished drawing the bricks, say: "Work with your group to think of reasons you might separate yourselves from the people on the other side of the "pretend" wall. Write each reason on one of the bricks you have created. Do not refer to any specific persons and try to be general. Write inside as many bricks as possible."

Allow youth about five minutes to brainstorm and fill in the bricks. You may help if necessary. When they have finished, ask for a volunteer from each small group to read aloud some of his or her team's reasons. Have the volunteers read one at a time, alternating sides. Then ask:

- What have we created and what does it represent?
- Why do you think we drew a brick wall for this activity? How are the reasons you wrote on the paper bricks like bricks in a real wall?
- Which of these reasons for judging do you observe most often in your school? Why?
- What are some other barriers that people build between themselves and others?

Say: "This paper prevents us from seeing one another very well. How do judgments based on stereotypes and prejudices keep us from seeing others as Jesus sees them?" After hearing answers, say, "We're going to leave this paper between us as a reminder of the ways we judge and separate ourselves from others."

AND

zooming in

Provide a long sheet of paper (or tape together several large sheets of paper), masking tape, and markers.

Stretch a long piece of paper across the room and attach it to opposite walls. If possible, secure the paper at a height that will block one group's view of the other group.

Clean or Unclean? (5–10 minutes)

Provide Bibles.

Say: "Peter, one of Jesus' disciples, had been taught that some animals were clean and others were unclean. His belief was related to the ancient Hebrew understandings of what it meant to be a holy people who are consecrated to God. However, Peter's belief extended to his treatment of people. He believed some people were acceptable to God, while others were unacceptable and beyond God's grace. Eventually, though, Peter changed his mind."

Ask a volunteer to read aloud Acts 10:9-16, 28-35. Then ask:

- Who or what did Peter dislike or hate? (*pigs, camels, rabbits, fish without fins or scales, and persons who ate these animals*)
- Who or what have you been taught to dislike or hate (personal opinion)? Who taught you? (*family, peer, television, music, and so on*)
- What did Peter learn through his vision? (*God did not want him to treat persons as unclean or unworthy.*)
- How does this story apply to our world today? How does it apply to your daily lives?
- How does God treat people? (*God values all people and treats them equally.*)

Say: "God values and cares for all persons and treats us equally. Whenever you are tempted to judge people based on how they look, where they live, or their parents' careers, remember that God loves everyone—even people who are different from you."

refocusing

Journaling (5–10 minutes)

Provide student journals and pens.

Hand out student journals and allow the youth five to ten minutes to complete the activities on pages 12–15.

AND

Sending Forth (1–2 minutes)

Close the session in prayer. Then blow out the candle (lit during the opening activity) to signify that youth will go into the world, taking what they've learned everywhere they go. Encourage them to invite friends to the next session.

Too Bad You Don't Have What I Have!

Topic: Materialism; Haves and Have-nots

Scripture: Matthew 18:1-5

Key Verse: "Whoever becomes humble like this child is the greatest in the kingdom of heaven" (Matthew 18:4).

Take-Home Learning: Jesus calls us to be humble in the sight of God.

Younger Youth and the Topic

Today's youth cannot make it through a day without hearing or seeing messages that say: "Life is about the accumulation of stuff." Television is first and foremost a vehicle for advertisers to reach their desired demographic (and adolescents are near the top of that list). Movies are increasingly accepting product placements, and many theaters now run a series of commercials along with movie previews. Teen magazines boast stories and ads about the latest clothes, skateboards, make up, and electronics that youth "need." The truth is: Media glorifies gadgetry and good looks, sending the message to youth that what they have is more important than who they are. It's little wonder that younger youth come to believe equations such as these:

- Nice or trendy clothes = a cool person, probably popular
- Generic clothes = a nerd, possibly poor
- Baggy or unusual clothes = a troublemaker or loser

Like it or not, many youth view their world this way. Most of them will do anything to fit in and to be popular. Intellectually most youth know that what one has or doesn't have isn't important. But on a practical or emotional level, they only half believe this to be true. Regardless of their actual needs, what they really want and desire is to be accepted and to have what their friends, neighbors, and classmates have. However, once they reach this point, younger youth often want more: They want *better* stuff than their peers.

Your goal is to help youth want to live simply and to give what they don't need to the poor. Your challenge is to bring Christ to your youth "where they are," to help your youth hear Jesus' radical message for both the rich and poor, and to provide your youth an environment where God can work in their hearts.

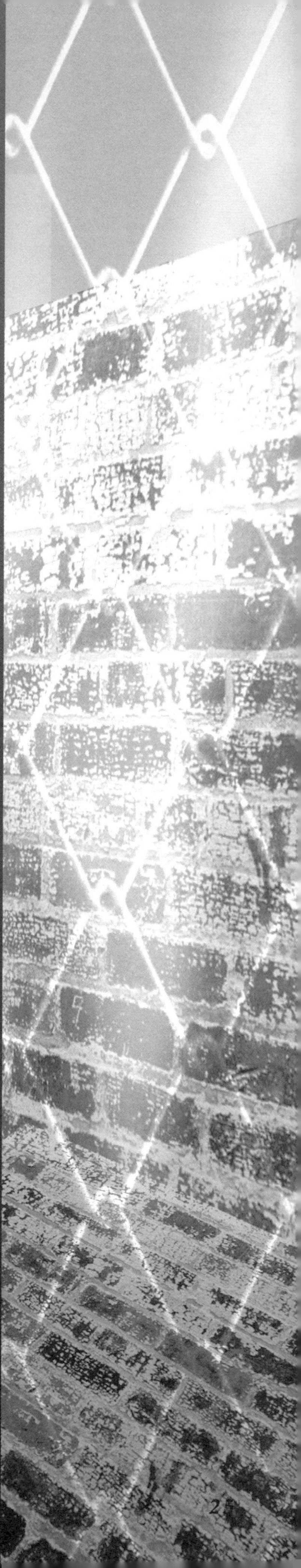

Theology and the Topic

In Jesus' culture, some religious leaders felt as if they had everything—power, job security, a good living—and they still lived faithfully according to the law. Many in Jesus' day believed that those who had possessions and good health were blessed by God. It follows then that those who were without these luxuries and comforts must have done something to anger God.

Though Jesus was poor, he was an artisan and a skilled tradesman—and he was not of the lowest social class—as were the destitute poor who were despised by many and roamed the streets begging for help. Jesus, however, lived by a different set of values. When Jesus' disciples asked him, "Who is the greatest in the kingdom of heaven?" Jesus answered, "Whoever becomes humble like this child is the greatest in the kingdom of heaven" (Matthew 18:1, 4). In the parable of the rich man and Lazarus (Luke 16:19-31), Jesus tells of a beggar covered with sores whom God elevates above the rich man "dressed in purple and in fine linen" who "feasted sumptuously every day." In his Sermon on the Plain Jesus says, "Blessed are you who are poor, for yours is the kingdom of God. Blessed are you who are hungry now, for you will be filled" (Luke 6:20b-21a). In each of these cases, Jesus completely reverses everyone's expectations!

What does Jesus' message mean for those of us who live in a world where all is not equal? What does it mean for those who truly have the most and live comfortably—sometimes luxuriously? Can anyone be considered the greatest while worrying about wearing clothes that are in style or anxiously awaiting one's next meal at an expensive restaurant or dreaming of owning a car that will make everyone jealous? It is easy for us to get caught up in believing that riches and status are signs of God's blessing on us or our nation. However, Jesus tells us repeatedly that we are blessed when we give of what we have. This does not mean we should become destitute by giving away all that we own. Rather, our calling is to identify with the poor by seeing them as children of God and to consider the well-being of others before personal material comforts.

You and the Scripture

Read and meditate on **Matthew 18:1-5**.

Take a trip back in time to your middle school or junior high days. What did you think you "had to have" to fit in or to be happy during that time?

What did your parents, teachers, pastors, or Sunday school teachers say about these wants? Were you angered, frustrated, or confused by their responses? Remember these emotions as you prepare, as you think about your youth, and as you pray.

Where are the stereotypes and barriers among your youth? Who are the "haves" and "have-nots" in your group? How can you break down some of these barriers?

As you pray, keep in mind what the Lord requires and values: "What does the Lord require of you but to do justice, and to love kindness, and to walk humbly with your God?" (Micah 6:8).

Too Bad You Don't Have What I Have!

Scripture: Matthew 18:1-5

Take-Home Learning: Jesus calls us to be humble in the sight of God.

indicates key activity. If time is limited, focus here.

activity	time	preparation	supplies
first glance			
What Matters Most Game	8–13 minutes	Duplicate and cut apart seven copies of What Matters Most Game cards on page 51.	Game cards, small prize (optional), a candle, matches
a second glance			
Material Collage	7–10 minutes	Gather teen magazines and newspapers, or visit websites frequented by youth and print out images that represent status.	Teen magazines and newspapers or website pictures, glue, two posterboards
zooming in			
A Lesson in Humility	8–12 minutes	Review Matthew 18:1-5.	Bibles
refocusing			
Who Am I?	10–14 minutes	No preparation necessary.	Student journals, pens or pencils
AND			
Sending Forth	4–6 minutes	No preparation necessary.	Student journals

first glance

Provide copies of What Matters Most game cards on page 51, a candle, and matches. (A small prize for the winner of the game is optional.)

Duplicate and cut apart seven copies of the game cards on page 51. (If your group is large, you may need to make additional copies.) Shuffle cards before using in the session.

Leader's Guide

What Matters Most Game (8–13 minutes)

As youth arrive, have them sit in a circle. When everyone is present, distribute cards, making sure that each youth has at least seven cards. (It is OK if some youth have one more card than others.)

Say: "I'm sure most of you would love to have one or more of the items printed on these cards. There are seven copies of each type of card distributed throughout the group. Look through the cards you've received and decide which of the items listed you most desire. When I say 'Go,' try to collect all seven cards for one of those items. You may do this by trading cards with one another. For example, if you are trying to get rid of two cards, say, 'Two' and look for someone else who wants to trade two cards, but don't show each other the cards when you trade. You may trade as many or as few cards as you choose. When you have collected all seven cards in a set or when you have collected five hundred points, say to the group, 'I win!' Are there any questions?"

Play the game until someone declares himself or herself the winner. Then have all participants total their points. Surprise youth by explaining that the winner is actually the person with the least amount of points. (If you choose, award a small prize to the winner.) Then ask:

- What items did you want to collect?
- Did anyone consider collecting the cards that were worth the least amount of points?
- What did the items worth the most points have in common? What did the items worth the least points have in common?
- Why do we sometimes value possessions and comfort more than helping other people or living simply?
- How would you answer if someone asked you, "What matters most in life?

Now gather the youth in a circle. (If you have a designated sacred space, gather in this area.) Place a "centering candle" in the middle of the circle. (Leave this candle lit for the remainder of the session.) Light the candle and pray:

Jesus, our Light that shines in the darkness,
we want to see you.
Help us to see you in all people—rich and poor, young and old, all colors and kinds.

Jesus, our Light that shines in the darkness,
we want to see you.
Reveal to us the things that so fill up our lives that there's no room left for you. Amen.

Material Collage (7–10 minutes)

Distribute newspapers and teen magazines and ask the youth to search for pictures, phrases, and images that represent status. Youth should look for those items that would make them feel as though they had "made it." Assure youth they will not have to talk about the pictures they choose. Direct individuals to cut out and glue the words and pictures to the same posterboard.

Then have the youth cut out stories, headlines, and pictures related to hunger, poverty, oppression, and anything else related to the "have-nots" of the world. Ask them to glue these to a second posterboard.

Allow about five minutes for work. When youth have finished, ask them to compare the two collages they have created. Then ask:

- What do you notice about the two collages?
- How are the two collages similar? different?
- Where do you see God in the collages?

Display the collages where youth can see them for the remainder of the session.

a second glance

Provide teen magazines (or magazines popular among teens), newspapers, glue, scissors, and two posterboards.

If you do not have access to teen magazines, check the websites frequented by youth and print out pictures and images that represent status.

A Lesson in Humility (8–12 minutes)

Say: "Just like us, Jesus' disciples had questions about greatness and what people really need in life. In fact, they not only asked about what made someone great on earth but also they asked what made someone the greatest in the kingdom of heaven!"

Gather the youth in a circle and ask for volunteers to roleplay the following from Matthew 18:1-5:

- Jesus' disciples: Like Jesus, these persons were artisans or trade persons and were relatively poor.
- A child: Since the child was right there, he or she was probably the child of a poor family or perhaps a beggar living on the street. He or she may even have been an orphan.
- Jesus: As a teacher, Jesus never fails to surprise his students.
- Narrator: One youth will read the non-speaking parts.

Tell the remaining youth that they will play the role of the crowd on the streets of Capernaum. Hand out Bibles and instruct students to read Matthew 18:1-5 before acting out the Scripture by playing their assigned roles. Encourage them to think about what the persons in the story were thinking and feeling when this story took place.

After the youth have roleplayed the Scripture, ask:

- How do you think the disciples felt when Jesus told them that

zooming in

Provide Bibles.

someone like a child from the streets was the greatest in the kingdom of heaven? Why? (*They were probably surprised or shocked by Jesus' statement.*)

- How do you think the child felt? Why?
- How do you think the crowd felt? Why? What are some of the different emotions that people may have experienced when Jesus said, "Whoever becomes humble like this child is the greatest in the kingdom of heaven"?
- What do you think Jesus meant when he told his disciples to be humble like the child? (*They should rethink their expectations of God's kingdom.*)
- What does this story say about how we should view and treat one another? (*The community of the people of God is made up of persons who are humble and who welcome the poor.*)

If time permits, read Matthew 19:13-15, another story about Jesus welcoming little children. (Judging by how the disciples act in this passage, they didn't hear a word Jesus said in Matthew 18:1-5!)

refocusing

Provide student journals and pens or pencils.

Who Am I? (10–14 minutes)

Hand out student journals and direct youth to the activities on pages 16–19. Have them complete the sentences on pages 16–17. After three to four minutes, ask any youth who wish to share:

- how they can be humble
- how their life could be perfect
- how they could become good enough for God

AND

Provide student journals and pens.

Sending Forth (4–6 minutes)

Close the session by allowing time for students to write the prayer on page 19 of their student journals. Let all who wish to read aloud their prayers. Then blow out the candle (lit during the opening activity) to signify that youth will go into the world, taking what they have learned everywhere they go.

If no one wants to share his or her prayer, pray this prayer:

"Gracious and loving God, you have given us enough stuff. But we know of others who are less fortunate than we are. Give us the strength of will to share our stuff with others. Help us stay focused on what matters most in this world—doing your will. Amen."

There's Enough for Everyone

Topic: Hunger and Poverty

Scriptures: Mark 6:34-44; 10:17-31b

Key Verse: "Jesus, looking at him, loved him and said, 'You lack one thing, go sell what you own, and give the money to the poor; and you will have treasure in heaven; then come, follow me'" (Mark 10:21).

Take-Home Learning: We are called to make wise choices with our money and to hear God's call to care for the poor.

Younger Youth and the Topic

Although children comprise our country's largest demographic of those living in poverty, most of the youth in your congregation are probably not poor. When younger youth are confronted with the reality of poverty, it can be extremely disconcerting for them. Their idealistic and fairly self-centered worldview doesn't leave a lot of room for the realities of those who live below or near the poverty line. Yet their idealism can be channeled into action, and often they bring enormous energy to projects that help the poor.

Where faith and service intersect, younger youth may be shocked—much like the rich man or the disciples when Jesus told them to go feed the five thousand. And just as did the disciples and the rich man, our students stand in the presence of God and lament: "I have to give up everything. Are you kidding?" Junior highers are yearning to know that God is reliable, and they seriously hope God won't shake up their lives too much. But living in this world while following God's will challenges our youth (and adults!).

The idea that they must give up their "stuff" in order to enter the kingdom of heaven is not only difficult for them but also seems downright impossible. Remember—society's message is that the stuff they have is what makes them important.

Theology and the Topic

Just as long ago Christ challenged all those who heard him, Christ challenges us to have enough faith to give up comfort. In a world with so many needs, God asks us the question: "What are you willing to give up so others can live?" When Jesus told his disciples to feed all those gathered, in essence he challenged their faith: "Is there enough for everyone?"

Too often we live out of the belief: "I got mine on my own; you must get yours on your own." This belief is a product of our individualistic culture and reveals that we often fail to fully place our trust and faith in God. The act of selling everything and giving to the poor, of giving all we have to give, forces us to rely on God. The rich man who asked Jesus about gaining eternal life believed he was doing all the law required. His reliance was not on God, but on himself. Jesus wanted the rich man to place his trust solely on God. Jesus wants the same from us.

You and the Scripture

Read **Mark 6:34-44; 10:17-31b.**

After reading the session background Scripture, answer the following questions:

- What do you hear in the words of today's key verse? How are you challenged by it?

- If Jesus had told the rich ruler: "Trust me fully and come follow me," would his words have had the same impact?

Identify those things that keep you from fully trusting God. Pray that your faith may be strengthened this week.

Be honest with yourself. Isn't it easier to put your trust in things than in God? As you prepare, think of what and who you trust. If you have put your faith in someone or something other than God, list it here.

- Is there something you could give up that would allow someone else to have food, clothing, or shelter?

- Thoreau once wrote, "Live simply that others might simply live." How is living simply an act of faith?

There's Enough for Everyone

Scripture: Mark 6:34-44; 10:17-31b

Take-Home Learning: We are called to make wise choices with our money and to hear God's call to care for the poor.

(key icon) indicates key activity. If time is limited, focus here.

activity	time	preparation	supplies
first glance			
Rag Tag	7–12 minutes	Set up an obstacle course in the church parking lot. Collect clothes for relay and two shopping carts.	Clothes for relay, two shopping carts, a stop watch (optional), candle, matches
a second glance			
(key) What's the Truth?	5–10 minutes	Duplicate copies of the Hunger Quiz on page 52. Attach a large sheet of paper to the wall.	Handouts, pens, calculators, large sheet of paper, markers, adding machine tape, masking tape
zooming in			
(key) Sell It All	10–14 minutes	No preparation necessary.	Bibles, paper, pens
AND			
(key) What Does God Want From Me?	5–10 minutes	No preparation necessary.	Student journals, pens
refocusing			
Our Next Step	8–15 minutes	Research mission needs in your community.	Posterboard, markers
AND			
Sending Forth	8–15 minutes	No preparation necessary.	Lists compiled in "Sell It All"

first glance

Provide an overcoat, suit coat, large pair of pants (to be worn over the youths' clothes), hats, gloves, a shopping cart or shopping bag for each team (see below), and a stop watch (if possible), candle, and matches.

Beforehand, set up an obstacle course in the church parking lot, yard, or gym. Use chairs, rope, benches, poles, cones, and so on to create a course that youth can navigate with the cart. If you do not have shopping carts, have them run without them or they can carry a paper shopping bag of old clothes.

a second glance

Provide copies of the Hunger Quiz on page 52, calculators, large sheet of paper, markers, adding machine tape, and masking tape.

Attach the large sheet of paper to the wall in the meeting room.

Rag Tag (7–12 minutes)

Divide students into two teams. (If you have a large group, use more than two teams.) Distribute clothes among teams. Explain that the object is for each entire team to run the obstacle course wearing the clothes. When you say "go," the first person in each line must put on the clothes (over his or her own) and push the cart through the course. Then he or she hands the clothes to the next person and continues relay-style until each person on the team has run the course. Time each team; the team who navigates the course in the shortest time wins.

Now gather the youth in a circle. (If you have a designated sacred space, gather in this area.) Place a "centering candle" in the middle of the circle. (Leave this candle lit for the remainder of the session.) Light the candle and open your session in prayer, remembering that Jesus promises to be anywhere that two or more are gathered. Pray:

> **Jesus, Light for our journey and Bread for our life, fill us with your peace.**
> **Give us strength to follow you—even when it's hard to do so.**
>
> **Jesus, Light for our journey and Bread for our life, fill us with your hope.**
> **May we be fed by you and share you with this hungry world. Amen.**

What's the Truth? (5–10 minutes)

Distribute copies of the Hunger Quiz on page 52 and allow several minutes for youth to answer questions. Then, as a group, go over the answers (on page 53). Ask:

- Which answers most surprised you? Why?
- Which of the answers motivated you to think? Why?

Give calculators to three youth. Ask one to determine approximately how many children die each day from hunger (*16,438*). Ask another to determine how many children die each hour from hunger (*685*). Ask a third youth to determine how many children will die in the next six years, if nothing is done to change this current rate of starvation (*thirty-six million*). Call on youth to state their answers, while you write them on a large sheet of paper. Then ask: "How do these numbers help you to think about the problem in a different way?"

Now pass out rolls of adding machine tape and markers. Ask the youth to work collectively to draw 685 stick figures. Tape these stick figures on the wall as permanent visual reminders.

Encourage youth to keep the questions and answers in mind while continuing today's Bible study. The youth may also need to continue working on drawing their stick figures as you move on to the Bible study.

Sell It All (10–14 minutes)

zooming in

Provide Bibles, paper, and pens.

Pass out Bibles, paper, and pens. Ask youth to list things that are most important to them. Then say and ask: "I'd like you to only *think* about the answer to the next question. Is there anything on your list that gets in the way of your relationship with God or with others? Circle those things on your list that answer the question. Then fold your paper and put it in a pocket."

Enlist several students to act out Mark 6:34-44. Build in a few minutes of brief practice before the presentation. Ask:

- How did the disciples react to Jesus' request to feed the people? (*Shock, distress, unsure, questioning*)
- What is our reaction when we are asked to trust God and sacrifice?
- Are we different from the disciples? What do you think this story tells us about God's care for the people of the world around us?

Ask one or more of the youth to read aloud Mark 10:17-31b while everyone else follows along. Then ask, "How is this story like the one we roleplayed earlier?"

Say: "The rich ruler wanted to be a follower of Jesus, but he loved his possessions and put his faith in them rather than Jesus. Jesus explained that the young man had to make a decision about what was most important to him. We are no different. We must make decisions about what is important in our lives. We can either feed ourselves or we can feed a world that's hungry in many ways."

Read aloud the following situations and ask students to think about what their responses would be if they put their faith in Christ.

1. Your grandmother has unexpectedly moved into your home. She cannot walk up and down the stairs very well, and she needs a bedroom on the first floor. The only first-floor bedroom is yours. You spent all summer creating the bedroom of your dreams. If you move upstairs, you will have to share a room. What would you do? What would be your attitude about the situation?
2. You have been saving your money for several months to buy some clothes you really want. You now have enough money to purchase the clothes. You've already told all your friends that you are going shopping this weekend. Your church newsletter arrives in the mail and you read about a special offering being collected to help a family who lost its home in a fire. What will you do? What would be your attitude about that choice?

Ask youth to recall situations in their own lives when they had to make choices. What choices did they make? Were the choices difficult? Then ask:

- What do today's Scriptures tell us about the choices that we make?
- What does it mean to make sacrifices? In what way does our faith in God affect our choices and sacrifices?

AND

What Does God Want From Me? (5–10 minutes)

Provide student journals and pens.

Pass out the student journals and pens. Allow students to find a quiet spot in the room to reflect, think, and pray before turning to pages 20–21 and reflecting on today's session. Encourage youth to pay close attention to their feelings and emotions as they answer the questions related to living out their faith.

refocusing

Provide posterboard and markers.

Ahead of time, research possible mission needs in your community.

Our Next Step (8–15 minutes)

Begin by asking, "What can we do as a group to help feed others?" If possible, present some current mission needs through your denomination's website, or check with agencies in your community that offer food programs of various kinds. Also consider sponsoring a child from an organization such as Compassion International.

Provide time for youth to choose a project and to brainstorm ways to raise money. They may wish to conduct a fundraiser, or they may simply choose to set aside a certain percentage of their income for a month. Ask youth to create a poster that identifies their commitment, and ask those who are willing to commit to the project to sign their names on the poster.

AND

Sending Forth (1–2 minutes)

Ask youth to take out the lists they made earlier in "Sell It All." As you close the session with prayer, suggest youth look at their lists and ask for God's guidance in choosing their priorities. Blow out the candle (lit in the opening activity) to signify that the youth are to take the light of Jesus and all that they have learned everywhere they go.

In My Own Backyard

Topic: Mission and Service Opportunities

Scripture: John 15:1-8; James 2:14-18

Key Verse: "But someone will say, 'You have faith and I have works.' Show me your faith apart from your works, and I by my works will show you my faith" (James 2:18).

Take-Home Learning: We are called to bear the fruit of good works in the world.

Youth and the Scripture

"Youth don't care about their world. Youth think only about themselves."

Unfortunately, adults often bring these charges against today's youth. Statements such as these sell the younger generation short. By accusing youth of being selfish or apathetic, we imply that they are incapable of being mission-minded or that they are unable to serve as the hands and feet of Christ. Yet when given the opportunity, younger youth are more than capable of living out their faith. Adults must remember that youth often have a "simple" faith; it is unfair to expect them to have a mature, complex faith. Unfortunately, when younger youth fail to live up to our expectations, their actions may be dismissed as insincere attempts to live out their faith.

Younger youth are just beginning to connect their faith to their everyday lives. They have a tendency to avoid or even abandon that which appears to have little personal value or be too difficult. When youth are expected to "be just like Jesus," to never laugh at their friends or talk about others behind their backs, and to give all they have to the poor, they are measured against a standard that few, if any, Christians could meet.

Instead of demanding perfection, praise your youth for the little steps they take that make a difference in their world. Remember that they are on journeys of faith—and haven't yet arrived. As John Wesley said, We are are going on to perfection. Your youth are taking steps toward showing their faith through their works. Since they sometimes take as many steps backward as forward, remind them that they are not alone on their journeys. God—and you—will walk by their sides.

Theology and the Topic

James poses a question that Christians have been struggling with for centuries: Which is more important: faith or works? As Jesus' first followers were learning what it meant to be Christians, they debated how to best express their faith. In James 2:14-26, James argues that our actions prove our faith, even saying, "Faith by itself, if it has no works, is dead" (James 2:17). He also reminds us that Jesus' life was one of action. Remember the many ways Jesus put his faith into action—touching, teaching, talking, praying. He instructed his disciples to do the same.

In John 15:1-8, Jesus compares his followers to a vine's fruit-bearing branches. How does one know that a vine is alive and vital? By the fruit that it bears. Likewise, others will know our faith is alive and vital if our actions show it.

At the core of these two Scriptures is an important understanding of the Christian life. Just as we become self-centered when we dwell on our possessions, our time, our work, and so on, our faith also can become self-centered. The danger is sticking "too close to the vine," focusing on our spiritual needs to the point that we neglect to turn our attention outward. If our faith fails to feed others as well as ourselves, it is not fully life-giving.

You and the Scripture

Read **John 15:1-8 and James 2:14-18.**

How do you feel about the relationship between faith and works? How important is it to you that others see or experience your faith through your actions? How important is it that others know about your faith through your words? In the space below, record your thoughts and feelings about faith and works:

- In what actions (works) do you engage that are primarily motivated by your faith?

- How do your works help others experience Christ in the world?

In My Own Backyard

Scripture: John 15:1-8; James 2:14-18

Take-Home Learning: We are called to bear the fruit of good works in the world.

indicates key activity. If time is limited, focus here.

activity	time	preparation	supplies
first glance			
Tree of Faith	5–10 minutes	Duplicate the Tree of Faith on page 54.	Handouts, markers, candle, matches
a second glance			
Act It Out	10–15 minutes	Acquire a list of homebound and hospitalized church members. Check church-kitchen supplies.	List of homebound and hospitalized church members, baking supplies, art supplies, wax paper, paper sacks
zooming in			
Faith Is a Verb	15–20 minutes	Invite one guest speaker to talk to the youth about gardening and another to talk about mission work.	Guest speakers, Bibles, a marker board or large sheet of paper, marker
AND			
Right in Our Own Backyards	8–12 minutes	Determine community needs.	Large sheets of paper, markers
refocusing			
An Action Plan	4–8 minutes	No preparation necessary.	Student journals and pens
AND			
Sending Forth	1–2 minutes	No preparation necessary.	No supplies

first glance

Provide Tree of Faith handout on page 54, markers, a candle, and matches.

Duplicate copies of the Tree of Faith handout on page 54.

a second glance

Provide a list of shut-ins, hospitalized members, and members living in retirement centers; brownie and/or cookie mix; baking supplies; art supplies for making cards; wax paper; and paper sacks.

Request from your church office a list of shut-ins, hospitalized members, and/or members who live in a retirement center. Ask for information about these persons such as interests, likes and dislikes, families, and so on.

Also make arrangements to use the church kitchen.

Tree of Faith (5–10 minutes)

As youth arrive, distribute copies of the Tree of Faith handout on page 54. Then ask them to write on the roots some of the ways that Christians "learn" their faith. (*For example: attending worship, reading Scripture, being in fellowship with other Christians, and so forth.*) Then ask them to write on the leaves some of the ways that Christians "show" their faith. (*For example: visiting nursing homes, collecting canned foods, being kind to others.*) Encourage creativity.

Now gather the youth in a circle. (If you have a designated sacred space, gather in this area.) Place a "centering candle" in the middle of the circle. (Leave this candle lit for the remainder of the session.) Light the candle and pray:

Jesus, come and illuminate our lives. Give us new eyes to see the needs of the world around us.

Jesus, come and illuminate our lives. May others come to know the face of Christ as you shine through each of our actions in the world. Amen.

Act It Out (10–15 minutes, not including baking time)

If your church has a kitchen, gather there to complete this activity. Using brownie mix and baking supplies, work with the students to bake batches of brownies and cookies. Depending on the size of your group and your church's facilities, you may need to divide the youth into small groups. Be sure to carefully follow the directions on the package.

As the brownies and cookies are baking, ask youth to create "thinking of you" cards for the hospitalized or homebound members.

After the cookies and brownies have baked and cooled, wrap them in wax paper, place in paper sacks, and attach a card to each bag. If possible, plan a time during the week to deliver the bags and cards.

Faith Is a Verb (15–20 minutes)

Introduce your two guests and briefly explain the purpose in their visit. (See margin note on page 41.)

After the guests have spoken and made any presentations, divide the youth into two groups. (Invite your guests to join one of the two groups or assure them they may leave if they need to return to their own classes.) Ask the first group to read John 15:1-8 and answer the following questions:

- In this Scripture, who is the vine? Who are the branches?
- What does it mean for the branches to bear fruit?
- What does it mean for God to prune the branches so they can bear more fruit?

Ask the second group to read James 2:14-18 and to answer the questions below. You may want to suggest this group read the passage from *The Message* on page 26 of the student journal.

- In your own words, define *faith*.
- What does James mean by "works"?
- What is the relationship between faith and works?
- How would life be different if everyone lived entirely by faith? by works?

Wait a few minutes for groups to read the Scripture passages and to discuss answers. Then ask a representative from each group to present answers. Ask:

- How do these two Scriptures relate to each other?
- How do they relate to the Tree of Faith created earlier?

AND

Right in Our Own Backyards (8–12 minutes)

Divide the youth into small groups of three or four. Give each group a large sheet of paper and a marker and direct each to divide the paper into three columns labeled: *Need, What It Would Take, and How We Can Help.*

Then say: "Often we tend to focus on mission projects that have a big impact, such as feeding the hungry, ensuring education for children in third world countries, or helping communities to rebuild after devastating floods, hurricanes, or tornados. These projects are extremely important and require the time and effort of many people. At the same time, we sometimes overlook the many smaller but very real needs right here in our own community. I want each group to concentrate on one aspect of our community that has needs. List some of these needs in the first column. Then talk about how each need could be met and list solutions in the second column. Finally, discuss what you can do in response to each need and record in the third column. For example, suppose you determine that elderly persons need help with their yard work. You might decide that a list of volunteers willing to do the yard work would solve the problem, and youth can help by raking leaves or mowing lawns."

Assign each group one aspect of your community that has needs. (See suggestions listed in the margin on page 42.) After about five minutes of work, ask group representatives to present their ideas.

zooming in

Provide guest speakers, Bibles, a marker board or large sheet of paper, and a marker.

Invite an avid gardener to speak to your group about why he or she likes to garden. Also ask this gardener to bring a potted plant and demonstrate proper plant care, particularly pruning (John 15:2).

Additionally invite a church member who has participated in a mission trip to tell about his or her experience. Ask this person to describe how the mission experience connected with his or her faith.

Copy the two sets of questions on a marker board or large sheet of paper.

Provide large sheets of paper and markers.

Suggested Categories:

- The elderly
- Young children
- Those living in poverty
- Those who are homeless
- The environment
- Schools
- Health and safety issues

refocusing

Provide student journals and pens.

Ask:

- If you had to choose one need for our large group to address, what would it be? (If there is consensus on this question, start making plans!)
- For each of these needs, you determined a possible solution. What keeps us from doing what we can to help? (*Possible answers: We're too busy; we're too focused on our own needs and wants.*)
- What do these needs have to do with our faith? How does our faith prompt us to respond to these needs?

An Action Plan (4–8 minutes)

Hand out student journals and pens. Read aloud James 2:18. Suggest youth move to quiet spots and complete the activities on pages 24–27 in the student journal.

AND

Sending Forth (1–2 minutes)

Gather the youth in a circle. Ask each youth to say aloud one thing they will do this week to live out his or her faith. Then close the session by praying that God will guide the youth to better see and respond to the needs around them. Blow out the candle (lit in the opening activity) to signify that youth will go into the world, taking what they've learned everywhere they go.

1+1+1+1 Adds Up

Topic: Working Together As the Body of Christ

Scripture: 1 Corinthians 12

Key Verse: "But God has so arranged the body, giving the greater honor to the inferior member . . . If one member suffers, all suffer together with it; if one member is honored, all rejoice together with it" (1 Corinthians 12:24b, 26).

Take-Home Learning: Each person is just as important as another, and God has given us the gifts that we need to work together as the body of Christ.

Younger Youth and the Topic

By this age, youth have figured out that all are not equal in their world. The star athlete may receive special treatment at school. Talented musicians, artists, or actors may receive privileges not available to other students. Even in youth group, they may feel as if some of their peers are treated better than others. The bottom line is that youth feel great when *they* are at the top of the heap, but they don't feel so great when their individual weaknesses are evident to others.

Even when we have no intention of doing so, adults compare youth. When students hear an adult say something like "Why can't you act more like so and so," or "Look at how so and so is working—you need that kind of work ethic," they aren't motivated. Instead they feel inferior to their peers or that they are being held to an unfair standard. Teachers and youth leaders communicate subtle messages about youth by calling only on those students who seem especially interested in the material or by joking around after class with just a few youth. Though adult leaders rarely intend to pit one student against another or to make someone feel as though she or he is inferior, they can't always predict how youth may internalize their statements and actions.

With younger youth, our task is to help them understand what their gifts are and that each individual gift is important and useful. Younger teens are changing so rapidly that they need consistency in their lives. Through all the changes, it is important that they recognize that God has given them unique and needed gifts. Also, just as the person in the last chair of the clarinet section contributes to the total sound of the band, all gifts—even those that seem unimportant—contribute to the work of the body of Christ.

Theology and the Topic

In Paul's writings, we find that the church at Corinth is facing problems similar to those faced by many of today's congregations. The community was diverse both in its membership and in the gifts contributed by those members. Further, whereas leadership had once been the job of a chosen few, Paul was encouraging all Corinthians to discover and use their gifts in God's service. Unfortunately, the Corinthians did not understand that all of God's gifts are equally important. They fought among themselves about whose gifts were greater or more important in God's eyes.

In 1 Corinthians 12, Paul uses the body as an analogy for how the members of the church should work together. Paul insists that no one person's gifts are greater than another's. Also no one knows why or how God decides the distribution of gifts. Paul challenges Christians to acknowledge their own gifts without fretting over whose gifts are greater. Likewise, we are called to use our God-given individual gifts to the best of our abilities.

Even today this is a difficult task for Christians! In our congregations, we tend to value Sunday school teachers and musicians over cookie-bakers and dishwashers. Too often churches make ministry the job of a select few instead of incorporating the entire body. Paul's talk of gifts is meant to encourage and strengthen us, but using our gifts as God intended can be frightening. Encourage your youth to value both their gifts and everyone else's in the church they call home.

You and the Scripture

Read and meditate on **1 Corinthians 12**.

God has given us individual gifts. Our task is to discover and use them. As you prepare for this session, identify the gifts you observe in your youth. Then identify the gifts God has given you that help you in your work with these youth. List these gifts below:

What gifts do others see in you? List these below. Compare this list to the list above.

Pray for your group and remember that God calls us to be humble. Changing the world often involves making personal changes first. What changes could you make that would help you make a difference in the world around you?

1 + 1 + 1 + 1 Adds Up

Scripture: 1 Corinthians 12

Take-Home Learning: Each person is just as important as another, and God has given us the gifts that we need to work together as the body of Christ.

(key icon) indicates key activity. If time is limited, focus here.

activity	time	preparation	supplies
first glance			
(key) Can We Get it Done?	6–12 minutes	Build an obstacle course, preferably outside or in your church's fellowship hall.	"Obstacles," strips of cloth, a candle, matches
OR			
Parts of the Body	6–12 minutes	Print 1 Corinthians 12:27-31 on a large sheet of paper and cut into nine puzzle pieces.	Twister® game, large sheet of paper, scissors, marker, candle, matches
a second glance			
(key) One Body Collage	8–12 minutes	Review 1 Corinthians 12.	Large sheets of paper, scissors, tape or glue, construction paper, magazines, newspapers
zooming in			
(key) Analogy Affirmation	10–20 minutes	Cut one slip of paper for each student.	Slips of paper, a container (bowl or basket), Bibles, student journals (optional)
refocusing			
Using My Gifts	5–10 minutes	No preparation necessary.	Student journals, pens
AND			
My Gift to God	4–6 minutes	Duplicate and cut apart the My Gift to God cards on page 55. Gift wrap a shoebox, leaving a small opening in the top.	Handouts, container (basket or bowl), shoebox, wrapping paper, tape, student journals, pens

first glance

Provide "obstacles" (tables and chairs work well), strips of cloth to make blindfolds, slings and to tie legs together, a candle, and matches.

Use old socks, hose, T-shirts, or sheets to cut into strips of cloth.

Set up an obstacle course (outside if possible) using chairs, tables, and other items. Use signs or masking tape to indicate pathways. Do not allow students to see the course ahead of time.

Conditions:

- Blind (wear a blindfold)
- Broken arm (wear a sling)
- Cannot use legs (tie legs together)
- Mute (cannot speak)

Provide a Twister® game, puzzle pieces, a candle, and matches.

Print 1 Corinthians 12:27-31 on a large sheet of paper. Cut the paper into nine puzzle pieces. Place each piece on one circle of the Twister® mat.

a second glance

Provide at least six large sheets of paper, construction paper, magazines, and newspapers.

Leader's Guide

Can We Get It Done? (6–12 minutes)

Gather youth together away from the obstacle course and assign each one of the conditions listed in the margin. (It is OK if the same condition is assigned to more than one youth.)

When everyone has arrived and has been "prepared" with a condition, lead them to the obstacle course. Say: "Work together as a group to move everyone through the entire obstacle course. Remember that each of you has restrictions that will make moving through the course more difficult."

After the youth have completed the obstacle course, ask them to reflect on the experience and if it was difficult asking for help.

Then gather the youth in a circle. (If you have a designated sacred space, gather in this area.) Place a "centering candle" in the middle of the circle. (Leave this candle lit for the remainder of the session.) Light the candle and pray:

Jesus, you are our source of light. Just as a candle can't burn without oxygen, we cannot thrive without being close to you.

Jesus, you are our source of light. Just as one candle can light up a dark room, so can we bring light to this world when we let your light shine through us. Amen.

OR

Parts of the Body (6–12 minutes)

Play Twister® using the standard rules. Whenever someone places a hand on a circle with a puzzle piece, that person should keep the puzzle piece. Play until you have a winner. (If all of the puzzle pieces have not been retrieved, you may want to play a second game.) Assemble the puzzle and read aloud the Scripture in unison.

Gather the youth in a circle. (If you have a designated sacred space, gather in this area.) Place a "centering candle" in the middle of the circle. (Leave this candle lit for the remainder of the session.) Light the candle and pray the centering prayer printed above.

One Body Collage (8–12 minutes)

Work together to cover a table or large area of a wall with large sheets of paper. Draw an outline of a person on the paper. (You might ask an artistically inclined youth to do the honors, or trace the body of one of your youth.) Give each student a sheet of construction paper along with old magazines and newspapers.

Ask the youth to find and cut out pictures, words, and phrases that represent their gifts and talents. Instruct them to use the construction paper to make a collage out of these pictures, words, and phrases. As the youth finish their collages, ask them to tape or glue their work inside the body outline. (Don't worry if some overlap or reach outside of the lines.)

When everyone has posted his or her collage, ask the youth to step back and look at the body they have created. Then ask:

- What do you notice about this body? What stands out?
- What would happen to our creation if we removed any one sheet of construction paper?
- Are any two collages exactly the same? What makes each collage unique?
- How is this project like the church?

Analogy Affirmation (10–20 minutes)

Distribute a small slip of paper to each youth (including yourself). Ask each to write his or her name on the slip and to place it in the container. Shake up the slips, draw one, and say: "We've come to know one another at church, but we don't often take the time to affirm the unique qualities we see in one another. I'd like you to imagine our group is a car and that each one of us is a part of that car. For example, someone who is good at supporting their friends might be seen as a tire, or a person with a lot of energy might be a battery. As I call out each name, tell that person what car part you think she or he most resembles and why. It's OK if more than one car part fits a particular person."

Refer youth to "Our Group As a Car: (Auto) Body of Christ" on pages 28–29 in the student journal. Draw the first name and invite youth to suggest car parts and reasons. When all of the names have been read aloud, ask:

- What do you think is the most important part of a car? Why?
- What parts do people tend to care for more than others?
- What happens to a car when one part is not working properly?

Say: "Early Christians often disagreed about what spiritual gifts were most important and useful. So Paul wrote to them and provided helpful advice. Let's take a look at it."

Hand out Bibles and ask for volunteers to take turns reading aloud 1 Corinthians 12 while the others follow along. Then ask:

- Why is it sometimes difficult to know what gifts God has given you?

zooming in

Provide slips of paper, a container (basket or bowl), scissors, and Bibles. (Student journals are optional.)

Cut apart as many small slips of paper as you expect youth to attend.

- Do you sometimes think that someone else's gifts are more important than yours? Why?
- What gifts do you wish you had been given?
- How are your gifts important to the church?
- What parts of the body are most important? What does Paul say about which of our gifts are most important?
- What does this Scripture have to say about the church? What does it say about how Christians can make a difference in the world?

refocusing

Provide student journals and pens.

Using My Gifts (5–10 minutes)

Hand out the student journals and instruct youth to complete the activities on pages 30–31. If time permits, allow youth to discuss their work in groups of three or four.

AND

Provide My Gift to God cards on page 55, scissors, a container (bowl or basket), a shoebox, wrapping paper, tape, student journals, and pens.

Cut apart the cards on page 55 and place in a container (bowl or basket). (If you have a large group, you may need to duplicate several copies and cut apart. Also gift wrap a shoebox and leave a small opening in the top.

My Gift to God (4–6 minutes)

Ask each youth to draw one card from the container and read the gift or quality listed. Then instruct students to reflect on this specific gift, making any personal notes of ways they might practice this gift on page 32 in the student journal.

Place the gift-wrapped box near the centering candle. Ask the youth to place their cards into the box, symbolizing their promise to use these particular gifts for God during the week.

Close in prayer, then blow out the candle (lit earlier in the session) to signify that youth are called to transform God's world using their gifts.

Environmental Match

Find others who can honestly answer "yes" to the actions in the boxes. No person may sign more than three times (unless you've asked everyone else in the room first).

Someone who has worn "hand-me-down" clothing	Someone who has shopped at a second-hand store	Someone who uses rechargeable batteries	Someone who has a solar-powered calculator	Someone who prints on both sides of computer paper.
Someone who recycles soda cans/bottles	Someone who uses reusable grocery bags	Someone who can name two environmentally friendly sources of energy/power	Someone who eats vegetarian at least once per week	Someone who can name two ways to save power at home
Someone who can name three sources of pollution	Someone who carpools more than once a week	**FREE SPACE**	Someone who grows a garden	Someone who knows personally someone who gardens
Someone who makes compost	Some one who uses a mulching lawn mower	Someone who has planted a tree	Someone who can name two beneficial insects	Someone who can name the three R's
Someone who recycles plastic containers (laundry detergent, milk cartons, and so on)	Someone who recycles cardboard	Someone who uses recycled paper	Someone who rides his or her bike or walks to school	Someone who recycles canned food cans

Session 2 Reproducible Page

Take a Look

Did you walk to church today?	Yes	or	No
Did you carpool to church today?	Yes	or	No
Is there a compost pile for use on the flowers and plants?	Yes	or	No
Are the lights on or off in areas not presently being used?	Yes	or	No
Does your church use recycled paper towels?	Yes	or	No
Does your church use recycled toilet paper	Yes	or	No
Does your church use recycled paper for bulletins and newsletters	Yes	or	No
Are there doors/windows open while heat or air conditioning is running?	Yes	or	No
Are the thermostats programmable?	Yes	or	No

How many recycling bins are on your church property? ______________________________

Do you use florescent or incandescent bulbs? ______________________________

What is the water-heater temperature? ______________________________

Are there dripping faucets anywhere? If so, where? ______________________________

Have someone who walked to church today sign here. ______________________

Have someone who carpooled to church today sign here. ______________________

Note any other environmentally-related problems you find below:

Session 2 Reproducible Page

What Matters Most Cards

100 $1000 Shopping Spree 100	90 New Sports Car 90
80 Used Car That Runs 80	70 Brand New Wardrobe 70
60 New Designer Jeans 60	50 New Cell Phone 50
40 Day Off From School to Work at Food Bank 40	30 Bicycle to Ride to and From School 30
20 Second-hand Clothes 20	10 Mission Trip With Youth Group 10

Session 4 Reproducible Page

Hunger Quiz

Instructions: Circle **True** or **False** for each question.

1. Each day approximately three million children under the age of five die in the world from hunger.

True or False

2. In the United States eight million people go hungry regularly.

True or False

3. Hunger and poverty only affect certain people, especially those in Africa.

True or False

4. People can work full-time and still live in poverty.

True or False

5. There is not enough food produced in the world to end hunger.

True or False

6. Malnutrition doesn't affect learning.

True or False

Answers to Hunger Quiz

1. **False.** The reality is that over six million children in the world die from hunger every year and will never reach their sixth birthday. (State of Food Insecurity in the World 2002. Food and Agriculture Organization of the United Nations. *http://www.fao.org/docrep/005/y7352e/y7352e00.htm*)

2. **False.** 33.6 million people, including 13 million children, live in households that experience hunger. This represents approximately 1 in 10 households in the United States. (Household Food Security in the United States, 2001. ERS Food Assistance and Nutrition Research Report No. FANRR-29, United States Department of Agriculture, October 2002. *http://www.ers.usda.gov/publications/fanrr29/*)

3. **False.** The face of hunger is: the older couple who has worked hard their entire lives only to find their savings wiped out by unavoidable medical bills; a single mother who has to choose whether the salary from her minimum wage job will go to buy food or pay the rent; a child who struggles to concentrate on his schoolwork because his family couldn't afford dinner the night before. (*http://www.bread.org/hungerbasics/faq.html*)

4. **True.** There are various reasons many working Americans are unable to feed their families. From a broader economic perspective, we can point to the fact that the United States has the highest wage inequality of any industrialized nation (Hunger in a Global Economy: Hunger 1998, Bread for the World Institute). People can work full-time, low-skill jobs and still not make enough money to maintain a basic standard of living to buy food, pay their rent and medical bills, buy clothes for their children and afford a car to transport them to work.

   Just providing food seldom gets to the roots of hunger. In the United States, food pantries provide urgently needed help. But food assistance is less important to overcoming hunger than job opportunities. Empowering people, providing them with opportunities, or helping them cultivate an awareness of what they can do to improve their lives is one of the most important ways of overcoming hunger and poverty. (*http://www.bread.org/hungerbasics/faq.html*)

5. **False.** Hunger does not exist because the world does not produce enough food. We have the experience and the technology to end the problem. The challenge we face is not production of food and wealth but a more equitable distribution. *(http://www.bread.org/hungerbasics/faq.html)*

6. **False.** Children attending school who have skipped one or more meals a day over a period of time suffer from malnutrition which affects how well their brains process and store information. Also it is difficult to concentrate on learning when a child's focus is on his or her empty stomach. We have long known that the minds and bodies of small children need adequate food to develop properly. But science is just beginning to understand the full extent of this relationship.

   As late as the 1980's, conventional wisdom held that only the most severe forms of malnutrition actually alter brain development. The latest empirical evidence, however, shows that even relatively "mild" undernutrition—the type of hunger we have in the United States—produces cognitive impairments in children that can last a lifetime. (Dr. J. Larry Brown, director of the Center on Hunger, Poverty and Nutrition Policy at Tufts University. *http://www.bread.org/hungerbasics/faq.html)*

Tree of Faith

Session 6 Reproducible Page

My Gift to God Cards

RESPECT	HONESTY	UNDERSTANDING	WARMTH
LOVE	KINDNESS	ENDURANCE	ENERGY
COURAGE	MORALITY	FORGIVENESS	MUSICAL ABILITY
SPEAKING	GRACEFULNESS	PRECISION	ZEAL
CREATIVITY	HELPFULNESS	FORTITUDE	SINCERITY
SYMPATHY	EMPATHY	WISDOM	VALOR
LOYALTY	CONTENTMENT	PURITY	REVERENCE
COOPERATION	REASONING	OPTIMISM	DEPENDABILITY
CONSISTENCY	PATIENCE	NATURALNESS	CONFIDENCE
GRACIOUSNESS	TENDERNESS	REFINEMENT	CALMNESS
SWEETNESS	SERENITY	ENCOURAGEMENT	PERSISTENCE
ADVOCACY	FAIRNESS	JOY	TEACHING
DELIGHT	DETERMINATION	SELF-CONTROL	COMPASSION

Session 7 Reproducible Page

Thinking About the Movie

Instructions: After watching the movie, underline the words below that describe how you feel. Add others if necessary.

Aggressive	Anxious	Apologetic	Arrogant
Bashful	Blissful	Bored	Cautious
Cold	Confident	Curious	Determined
Disappointed	Disbelieving	Enraged	Envious
Exhausted	Frightened	Frustrated	Guilty
Happy	Horrified	Hot	Hurt
Hysterical	Indifferent	Interested	Jealous
Lonely	Negative	Regretful	Relieved
Sad	Satisfied	Surprised	
Suspicious			
Undecided			
Add others:	____________	____________	

If my face showed how I feel, everyone would see:
(Draw your face in the space below.)

My prayer for the world and my prayer for me is:

Dear God,

“Making a Difference in the World” Retreat

Purpose: To spend intensive time learning and reflecting on ways in which students can become persons who are empowered to transform the world according to God’s call.

Preparation: Several weeks before the retreat, enlist a small group of adults and youth as the leadership team. This team should:

- choose a location for the retreat that is close in proximity to a shopping mall or area frequented by people of varied walks of life. Make sure the site has electricity for watching movies and listening to music.
- determine rules for the community and establish a working “Covenant for Living in Community. Be creative; for example, you might pattern it after the Ten Commandments.
- determine the cost of the retreat.
- decide how small groups will be divided.
- schedule chore rotation and other housekeeping items.[a]
- preview the movie. As they watch, suggest they note appropriate discussion questions as well as Bible verses in preparation for leading the discussions.

Provide registration and permission forms and copies of the “Covenant for Living in Community” to parents and students. Send a letter to parents explaining the purpose of the retreat and the schedule. Also explain that the retreat will be structured around the movie *Pay It Forward.* (See the Video Viewing Note on page 61.) Ask parents to read the covenant with their youth and have each youth sign and return it with the other forms. Set a registration deadline that will leave you adequate time to finish the planning. Once the students have registered, provide them with a “what to bring list.” Also include a list from a local agency that collects canned goods, toiletries, or other items. Ask students to bring at least one item on this list to the retreat. (See page 62.) Plan to provide extra Bibles and journals for friends of students who may attend the retreat.

Nametags

Trace handprints on different colors of construction paper. Use different colors to designate small groups. Pre-print students’ names on the hands to ensure they are readable and cover them with contact paper. Punch holes in the hands and string with yarn so the nametags may be worn around participants’ necks.

SUPPLIES:

- Bibles (one per student)
- Student journals
- pens and pencils
- markers
- CD player
- background music
- music for worship
- nametags
- posterboard
- VCR/ TV
- *Pay It Forward* movie
- paper hole punch
- yarn
- scissors
- tape
- large white candle
- posters finished during earlier session
- construction paper (various colors)
- contact paper
- large sheets of paper or marker board with markers
- modeling clay
- small votive candles and candle holders (one per youth)

FRIDAY NIGHT

6:00 **Welcome, Instructions, and Rules for Community**

6:30 **Dinner**

7:15 **Icebreakers**

8:00 **It's So Overwhelming**

9:00 **Movie Time: *Pay It Forward***

10:45 **Evening devotion**

FRIDAY NIGHT

Welcome; Instructions; Rules for Community

Allow time for students to settle into their rooms, then gather everyone together in the common area. Remind students of the covenant they signed and post a copy on the wall. Distribute chore lists and assignments. Answer all questions before dismissing for dinner.

Icebreakers

Play "get-to-know-you" games as a large group before dividing youth into pre-assigned groups. Explain that they will remain in these small groups throughout the retreat. Encourage group leaders to lead some small-group, get-acquainted activities before beginning the Bible study.

It's So Overwhelming

Give each small group a large piece of paper and markers. Ask each group to brainstorm what they think needs to be changed in the world. Allow 10–15 minutes for brainstorming. Encourage youth to list both serious and humorous items. Ask the small groups to share their lists with the larger group. Tape all of the sheets of paper together on the wall. Then ask the entire group: "Are there similarities? Are there differences?"

Instruct small groups to discuss the following questions:

- What it would be like and feel like to change the world?
- Can the world really be changed?
- Can one person change the world?

After 10–15 minutes, ask small groups to come together and share their thoughts and feelings as a large group.

The Movie: Pay It Forward

Prepare snacks. Gather youth together and say: "This movie will be the focus of the retreat. If you've seen the movie before, please try to view it as if you've never watched it. Think about your corner of the world."

When everyone is comfortable, watch the movie together.

Evening Devotion

Have the students gather in the holy space you have created for the weekend and light the Christ candle. Distribute the Thinking About the Movie handout on page 56. Ask the students to underline their feelings and to write a prayer to God while reflecting on the movie.

When everyone appears to be finished, form a circle and ask each youth to say one word that describes something for which they are truly thankful. Conclude by praying the Lord's Prayer together. (Remember to blow out the candle.)

SATURDAY

Morning Devotion

Gather in the holy space and light the Christ candle. Spend a few minutes singing praise songs or listen to praise songs from CDs.

Read aloud Micah 6:6-8. Turn to a partner and share how you can live out this verse today." Sing another song and close with prayer. Dismiss for breakfast.

Bible Study 1

Ask students to gather in their small groups and take their Bibles. Have each group read together Luke 6:17-23, 27-36. As a large group, watch the scene from the beginning of the movie where Trevor's mother confronts the teacher. In small groups, discuss the following questions:

- What made the mom so angry with the teacher?
- Is the teacher "out of line" with the assignment?
- Is this assignment different from Christ's expectation of us?
- Do you think God expects us to complete the task the teacher assigned?
- How does this Scripture fit with the teacher's assignment?

Reassemble and call on small groups to briefly share their discussions. Close by praying the Lord's Prayer together.

Free Time

Suggest that students play board games and listen to music. Provide crafts for students who may want to express their creativity. Encourage youth to interact with others during this time, but be mindful of any who may be feeling left out.

Field Trip

Explain to students that they will be going to a local mall (or similar setting) frequented by people from various walks of life). Once arriving at their destination, divide youth into their small groups for this activity. Ask

11:00	Head to rooms
11:30	Lights out
Saturday	
7:00	Wake up
7:45	Morning devotion
8:00	Breakfast
9:00	Bible Study 1
10:15	Free Time
12:00	Lunch
1:00	Prepare for and leave on field trip

them to observe different people interacting. In particular, they should:

- Identify the different types of people (according to race, economics, and so on)
- Notice if different people are treated differently
- Notice differences in the way people dress (Did they assume something about someone based on the way they looked or dressed?)
- Notice if they agree (disagree) with something they see or don't see
- Notice if anything they see makes them angry

4:00 Regroup and return to retreat site

Announce a time and place to meet after "people watching." When you return to the retreat site, spend time discussing what they observed on the field trip. Ask, "Is there anything you can do to make a difference in something you saw?" Dismiss for dinner.

5:00 Dinner

6:00 Bible Study 2

Bible Study 2

Direct youth to their small groups. Ask them to read Ephesians 4:1-7; 5:1-2. Then ask:

- What does Paul tell us about how to live with one another?
- What characteristics are we called to exhibit?

As a large group, watch the scene in the movie between the homeless man and the woman on the bridge. In small groups, discuss the following:

- Why do we often think that if someone does something nice for us they must want something?
- Must gifts or considerate actions have strings attached?
- How does looking at others first change our worldview?
- What would life be like if we always lived as though we owed someone (like a stranger) a favor?

How does this scene relate to the Scripture?

Encourage small groups to briefly share their discussions. Pray the Lord's Prayer together to close.

7:00 Clay Sculpting

Display the sculptures during closing worship.

Clay Sculpting

Ask youth to close their eyes and to listen and notice the images that come to mind as you read aloud Matthew 25:31-45. Now give students a chunk of clay each and ask them to express the Scripture's meaning using the clay.

Free Time

Allow those who would like to finish their sculptures to do so. Others may choose to work on other craft projects, play board games, be outside, sing, visit with one another, and so on.

Evening Devotion

Go to the holy space and light the Christ candle. Ask the students to approach three different people tell one thing they learned today. Then stand in a circle as a large group and ask each person to thank God for something that happened today. Pray the Lord's Prayer together as you close. (Remember to blow out the candle.)

SUNDAY

Bible Study 3

Direct students to gather in their small groups, making sure they have their Bibles. Ask them to read Micah 6:6-8 and Ephesians 5:1-2. Then as a large group, watch the movie scene that depicts the first day of school when the teacher gives the assignment and the discussion that follows. Ask:

- Why should we think about the world?
- What does the world expect of YOU?
- Does a project like this change how you view the world and other people?

Say: "As the teacher put it, the 'project requires an act of faith in others.' Do you agree or disagree?" Allow time for responses then ask, "What does Jesus say of this faith?"

Closing Worship

After everyone has packed, check to be sure the building is clean. Using the same small groups, instruct them to walk the grounds and collect any trash. When finished, gather for worship.

Use the worship service on pages 62–63 to close the retreat.

Video Viewing Note

When you show home videocassettes to a group of learners, you need to obtain a license to do so. You can get a public performance license (sometimes called a site or umbrella license) from The Motion Picture Licensing Corporation's church desk at 800-515-8855. The license is valid for twelve months and typically costs about $95. Check with your church, though, to see if an umbrella license has already been obtained. Often many denominations secure licenses for their churches.

8:30	Free time
10:30	Evening Devotion
11:00	Get ready for bed
11:30	Lights out
SUNDAY	
8:00	Wake up
9:00	Breakfast
10:00	Bible Study 3
11:00	Pack and clean up
11:45	Closing worship
12:45	Head for Home

Worship Service: Our Covenant to Make a Difference

Supplies for Worship: Bibles (including *The Message* by Eugene Peterson); clay sculptures (if available from the retreat); Christ candle; CD of Audio Adrenaline's "Hands and Feet"; paper and pencils; worshipful CD's; CD player; individual votive candles; Communion elements (if Communion is desired); liturgy written and displayed on large sheet of paper.

Remind students to bring their canned goods (or other items that were requested) to be used as part of the offering. Set up the worship space. On the altar, place the Christ candle as well as the clay sculptures. If Communion will be served, place the elements on the table.

Gathering

As the students gather, play a contemporary Christian or praise and worship CD. Ask them to focus on the scene displayed on the Lord's table. Welcome students and adult leaders to this time of worship, celebration, and covenant. Light the Christ candle.

Greeting

LEADER: God has called us to be his people.
ALL: We come to this place to worship.
Leader: God changes us and opens our hearts.
ALL: We cry out for the love of God in our lives.
LEADER: God challenges us to love the world.
ALL: We seek to show the world the love of God.

Opening Songs

"Bind Us Together" (*The Faith We Sing*, No. 2226)

"Gather Us In" (*The Faith We Sing*, No. 2236)

"Sanctuary" (*The Faith We Sing*, No. 2164)

Opening Prayer

LEADER: The Lord be with you.
ALL: **And also with you.**

Let us pray. God of changing lives, God of a hurting world, we come to worship and bring glory to your name. We seek to see your face in all who we meet, and we seek to be your hands and feet to the world. **Amen.**

Scripture

Read aloud Matthew 25:31-45 using the NRSV or NIV translation.

Music

Play the song "Hands and Feet" by Audio Adrenaline, asking youth to listen and pray as they hear the words and think about their relation to the Scripture.

Scripture

Read aloud Matthew 25:31-45 again, this time using *The Message*.

Response to the Word

Call on some of your student leaders to share their thoughts on the Scripture and how they believe God has called them to make a difference in the world. (You may want to arrange this ahead of time.)

Sing "The Summons" (*The Faith We Sing,* No. 2130).

Prayer of Confession

Pray: God, we are too quick to accept the world as it is. You have challenged us to make a difference in our world. We acknowledge that we do not put our full faith and trust in you.

Allow for a time of silent prayer and confession. Then say: "Through the grace of God in Jesus Christ you are forgiven." All respond: "Through the grace of God you are forgiven."

Making a Difference Offering

Play soft background music. Ask youth to list ways in which they are willing to make a difference in the world. Ask them to bring these along with their donations and place them on the Lord's table as their offering to God.

Communion

If you choose to celebrate Holy Communion, do so as your tradition requires. Allow the students to serve one another as a part of the covenant they are forming with one another and God.

Closing

Give each person a candle to take with them as a reminder of the covenant they made with God and one another to be the hands and feet of Christ for the world. Pray the Lord's Prayer together, then sing, "Shine, "Jesus, Shine" (*The Faith We Sing,* No. 2173).

Out and About: Help a Service Organization

Preparation

Survey your community and take an inventory of community needs. Contact a local homeless shelter, service organizations, free-lunch programs, battered-women's shelter, food pantry, and so on. Choose one or more places for students to participate in service opportunities. If possible, choose a location where youth have not worked previously.

Send a letter to the parents of the youth explaining the activity and the intended purpose. Be sure to complete the appropriate permission and liability forms. Also make arrangements for transportation to and from the activity.

Before the day of the outing, call the agency/organization you have selected and finalize the arrangements. Ask if the agency will provide someone to talk with the group about the agency's mission, the population that is served, and other information that would be helpful for your students. Purchase or secure any supplies needed for the project.

The Experience

As you gather, provide a nametag for each student. Stress the importance of becoming involved and working at whatever tasks are needed. Pray for your group and the work to be done before traveling to the site. On the way, encourage the students to ask questions.

Afterwards, debrief the experience by asking questions such as:

- What expectations or stereotypes did you have prior to the experience?
- Did the experience meet your expectations? Why or why not?
- What did you learn?
- Who did you talk to that made an impact on you?
- What did you learn from the conversation?

When the discussion is complete, provide a thank-you card for students to sign and mail it to the agency or organization. Pray together, thanking God for the experience of helping others.